LIFE REFLECTIONS

Create a Video Heirloom

By Pamela S. Clark and Janet R. Kinneberg

ISBN: 0989204707
ISBN-13: 9780989204705
Library of Congress Control Number: 2013908644
Parting Thoughts

ADVANCE PRAISE FOR *LIFE REFLECTIONS*

"This book targets the very basic practitioners, those who have minimal access to equipment and the editing process. The layout of the book is very direct and chronological; start here, do this, don't forget that, and wrap up the project this way."

—Don Walton, owner, *My Cherished Memories* video production

"They [the authors] share their insights in a warm and inviting way. Their love for what they do shines through on every page."

—Linda Newell, *published author and genealogist*

"This is a useful book for the amateur videographer. We were pleased to provide the technical consultation."

Mike Willhelm, *Videomaker Magazine*

"Patients who were able to participate in this process enjoyed creating a video that added permanence to their history. It is an honor to help patients fulfill this end of life wish for my patients".

—Twyla Norton, *Hospice Volunteer*

"A great primer for amateur videographers, and a motivational script for professionals to apply their craft within a personal family setting."

—Ken Ridgeway, former DP Videographer, *Hallmark*

"A theme that runs through the book is **Don't wait**! Don't wait to get better equipment, don't entertain any of the many excuses we have to procrastinate. Do it now while the window of opportunity is open. With hospice patients that window can close quickly and the opportunity to get their story is then lost forever. Memories fade—Don't wait."

—Lisa Campbell, *Draper Senior Center*

"The goal of palliative care is to improve quality of life for both the patient and the family. The process and result of recording their memories brings comfort to our patients."

—Kelly Fogarty, *Hospice Chaplain*

"This book is an absolute delight to read. It is practical, helpful, well-written and engaging, and it offers insights and wisdom the authors' gained through their own experience in creating treasured family heirlooms. Great job!

—Shannon Golub, *Curo Hospice*

ACCLAIM FOR RECORDING LIFE STORIES

"Creating an oral, written, or multimedia biography honors the life of your beloved. It allows him to share significant stories and transmit history and values to you and to future generations."

—Norine Dresser, *co-author of Saying*

Goodbye to Saying Goodbye to Someone You Love

"I urge you to pursue preserving your personal history to allow your children and grandchildren to know who you were as a child and what your hopes and dreams were.»

—Oprah Winfrey, *celebrity and philanthropist*

"I couldn't take my eyes off the screen. It was as if my mother was in the room with me. Watching the *Life Reflections* video is like having a favorite chat with my Mother, but one that never has to end."

—Lorie Ann Valley, *daughter*

To Lillian, whose love and smile light
up a small town. As our first "Star," she sparked our
passion for recording untold stories and
held our hands as we developed our craft.

And to Britten, whose grit and stalwart
courage inspired us to write this book and share
our mission with others.
Her parting thoughts of "carry on with what
makes you happy and it will be a beautiful ride"
inspire us daily.

Their Life Reflections are saved safely
on video and are forever etched in our hearts.

ACKNOWLEDGMENTS

We sit in awe of the health care professionals and hospice volunteers everywhere who dedicate their lives to helping those in need. They provide comfort to strangers as though they were family. We also thank the generous hospice patients and friends who have given us the greatest of gifts: their life stories.

We have been blessed with the support of many extraordinary people. Pamela would like to thank her parents for a lifetime of love and encouragement. Their mantra of "you can do anything" gave her the courage to attempt to write this book. Her sons, Colby and Connor, cheered the loudest for her when the book was finished. Most of all, she thanks her husband, Gary, who fed and watered the children while she wasn't looking and endured many one-track dinner discussions about "the book." Janet would like to thank her men, big and small—her husband Bill and their sons, Joe and David. They endured her numerous hours on the computer with patience and understanding. Janet also thanks her father for his lifelong grammar lessons and her mother for instilling an appreciation for a well told story. Family makes her world go 'round.

We are fortunate to have persuaded a number of people who are much smarter than us to read the manuscript in one form or another, and their insights and perspectives made writing and rewriting *Life Reflections Videos* a true joy. Many thanks to Britten Sadler, Don Walton (Creative Memories), Linda Newell, Lillian Bowlby, RitaRae Elsberry, Tyson Soffe (Jenkins–Soffe Mortuary), Kirsten Rocek, Janet Bigler, Ed Bigler, Janet Epson, and Nancy Morgan. We want to acknowledge all of the hospice administrators who have contributed to our on-the-job training, including Kit Jackson and Kelly Fogarty (Hospice for Utah), Shannon Golub (Curo Hospice), and the Utah Palliative and Hospice Organization Volunteer Committee. Our board of directors, composed of Maureen Henry, J.D. and Health and Aging Policy Fellow; Brent Bell, CPA; Kimberly Erickson; Kendall Sorenson–Clark (KSC Solutions); and Gary Clark, kept us true to our mission. Scott Jarrard and Robert Reed are talented freelance artists who helped us develop our corporate visual identity and to Steve Smith

(Verite.com) for designing the book's cover. Our deep appreciation goes to Doug Havens, Harry Cutting and Tom Hussey for contributing their amazing photographs. A special thanks to Mike Wilhelm at *Videomaker* magazine and Kenneth Ridgeway for their invaluable elucidation of all things technical.

CONTENTS

FOREWORD

The authors' path to creating the nonprofit Parting Thoughts company began when, as hospice volunteers, we recorded a Life Reflections video for a hospice patient. We have seen firsthand the positive effect that recording a video legacy has on a dying person. The sense of peace and relief that overcomes the person when the taping is finished inspires us to offer that release to others. It brings the patient comfort to know that his or her life will not be forgotten. One of the nurses said she believed her patient lived longer because he wanted to finish this important, final project. For us, it gave birth to a passion for capturing the stories of everyday people before it is too late.

> However many holy words you read, however many you speak, what good will they do you if you do not act upon them?
> ~Buddha

We began offering our service throughout the greater Salt Lake area, with the quest of introducing the Life Reflections method to others. Utahns are famous for discovering and documenting family, and a Life Reflections video becomes a family heirloom that greatly enhances those existing histories with a record of a person's core essence and spirit. We are constantly amazed at the responses to our "calling." Because every story is important, and every family cherishes the Life Reflections of their loved one after he or she is gone, the videos become a precious part of family memories.

We quickly realized, however, that we could not record all of the people who wanted to leave a moving picture history. So we set out to find a way to make it easy for anyone to make a Life Reflections video. This book, *Life Reflections Videos: Create a Video Heirloom*, is the result. It is a guide for family members and hospice volunteers to use in producing a video of their loved one's reflections about life.

Telling one's story is a profound and pleasing event. Regardless of age, everyone has a story to tell, and telling it in whatever way they wish gives the Star a form of immortality in their lifetime and after their death. For their children, grandchildren, friends, and neighbors, the Star's story will be a living and historical legacy.

INTRODUCTION

A Life Reflections video will preserve your family history in a new way—it reflects the *essence* of your aging parents or grandparents. Most of us have photo albums and scrapbooks documenting our family's milestones and history. These albums are typically thick books with carefully chosen photographs and memorablia, created with the hope of sharing memories for years to come. With the advent of new technology, video recording is an increasingly popular method for preserving family memories, too. The Life Reflections video is a single, thoughtfully crafted recording that spotlights the personality, spirit, and memories of a special person in your life. Such a treasured Life Refections video will find its place at the heart of your video scrapbook library and will enhance your family history collection.

> The Star is the person featured in the Life Reflections video. This special person might be a family member or a friend. He or she is the Star of your show.

We have designed *Life Reflections: Create a Video Heirloom* for the amateur videographer and family historian. This is a manual filled with the information we have gleaned while creating Life Reflections videos for dozens of senior citizens and hospice patients. We share the knowledge we have gained over the years that will help you to create your own Life Reflections video for your Star, who may be your family, your friend, or even yourself. In this guide, we refer often to your loved one as the Star. This is intentional because this life recording is "their story, told their way." Simply put, your loved one is the Star of your show.

Allow us to be your guide, and your production will be good—very good. Your video will become a treasured heirloom in your family. You can take pride in what you have done as you share the video with friends and family.

Our guide is organized in five straightforward chapters. Here is a brief preview of what is presented in each chapter:

Chapter 1: Starting Thoughts introduces you to the process of creating and saving video memories in a virtual video scrapbook that we believe will become a standard tool for all family historians. After reading Chapter 1, you will understand the importance of creating a Life Reflections video and be able to identify the recording equipment you will use and the editing path you will follow. Finally, it is important to consider how your video will be shared. These starting thoughts will shape your video into the masterpiece you have dreamed of.

We review the planning process in Chapter 2: Planning Over a Cup of Tea. This is a crucial step in organizing your project and engaging your loved one. This first planning discussion takes place in a cozy setting in which you sip tea and discuss the project. People love this step, and so will you.

The Planning Over a Cup of Tea pre-recording conversation is the time for you to get a good idea of what your Star wants to say, assess and make note of any background noises, and determine what photographs and memorabilia the Star should collect and bring to the interview. The worksheets at the end of this chapter help you structure the interview and make note of the production and setting details.

Chapter 3: Armchair Interview gives specific directions for creating the desired tone and atmosphere for the interview through the use of camera angles and the setting. An overview of camera framing and a checklist for removing distractions and noises is also included.

In Chapter 4: Audio and Lighting Matters, we review the technical concepts behind capturing quality video and audio. You can create acceptable video in your own home with your existing equipment, and we show you how.

Chapter 5: It's a Wrap! contains post-production editing options and ideas for sharing your video and archiving your treasure.

Chapter 6: Parting Thoughts includes a special section for hospice workers and volunteers and suggests the best options for their uniquely time-sensitive projects.

The trouble is, you think you have time.
~ Buddha

We explain our tried-and-true methods that will help you to produce a cherished Life Reflections video. You can build on this method, but start as simply as possible. This is how great projects grow and how we suggest you approach yours.

We recommend that you read chapters one through three and then take a break. You will face many decisions, and you will need to consider them carefully. We encourage you to use the worksheets at the end of each chapter to jot down questions and potential issues that arise for you, and then let the project steep for a day or two. Chapters four, five, and six should answer most of the your initial questions.

Keep this book handy as you create your "moving picture" masterpiece. It is our hope that you will be encouraged and emboldened with the knowledge that we are right by your side. It is our honor to share our experiences with you, and it is our fervent wish that by creating your video, "your faculties and talents come alive, and you discover yourself to be a greater person by far than you ever dreamed yourself to be."[1]

Chapter One:

STARTING THOUGHTS

Chapter One

STARTING THOUGHTS

There are two mistakes one can make along the road to truth...

not going all the way, and not starting.

~Buddha

Welcome to a new and exciting way of looking at a person's life and legacy—through the lens of a video camera. Life Reflections videos capture for generations yet to come the joyful sound of your mother's laughter and the treasured twinkle in your father's eye that are impossible to describe with words. Going far beyond static photographs and written biographies, Life Reflections echo the person's spirit. They capture moments in time, a small sample of a storied life, for your loved one to share with families and friends.

These priceless videos are an essential new tool for scrapbookers and family historians. Through thoughtful video recording, your Star will tell his or her story—his or her way. With today's recording technology and a little forethought, priceless generational links and personal anecdotes are preserved for "virtual" lifetimes. Life Reflections videos range from complex multimedia videos that may include music, digitized photographs, and text overlays to short, unedited video taken with a smartphone.

Life Review Videos Provide the Following:

• A highly prized supplement to photo albums and scrapbooks.

• A living legacy to future generations.

• The *Star* with comfort in the knowledge that he or she will not be forgotten.

Preserving a person's reflections of life serves many purposes. It is undoubtedly a highly prized memento that ensures a video legacy for future generations, but more importantly, creating this masterpiece provides comfort to the one making the recording. Your Star will be reassured that his or her life reflections are preserved for all those they love and all who love them in return.

According to Kirsti A. Dyer, a respected physician specializing in life challenges, loss, grief, and bereavement, "Forming a story about one's life experiences improves physical and mental health. Storytelling is a part of life, intrinsic to most cultures. They help people make sense of the world—life's experiences, dilemmas, and hardships. Stories can educate, inspire, and build rapport. They are a means of communicating, re-creating, and helping preserve cultures."[2]

Our goal is to guide you through the simplest method we know to video-record a Life Reflections heirloom. You can always build on this method, but simply *start*! As Homer said, "The journey is the thing."[3] By all means, keep your eyes on the prize, but have fun along the way.

Life Reflections Videos is a delightful, easy-to-follow book that was designed with the beginning video scrapbooker in mind. It is packed with systematic do-it-yourself instructions and tips to assist you through the entire process and to help you avoid potential pitfalls. We will walk you through the necessary steps to help you determine which tools will work best for your particular situation. Today is the day you begin your trek on the enlightening road to creating a cherished family treasure guaranteed to last lifetimes.

Approach with Grace: Honor the Star

Capturing the living color and emotion that are inherent to a person's life is a very intimate and private project that needs to be approached with grace. Your Star may reveal personal details as he or she reviews the past and speaks about his or her hopes for the future.

Your desire to record the personal stories of a loved one honors his or her life and memories. The recording process will undoubtedly become a mutually bonding experience, one that you both will treasure for the rest of your lives. Take a moment to consider your role in this project. We encourage you to keep your Star at the forefront of your planning. You may experience personal temptations and family pressures to mold this video to meet others' needs. Resist that urge; this is not about anyone's needs except your Star's.

Your "Star" deserves the best treatment possible.

Helping someone record his or her life story is not a type of therapy; however, your Star may find it curiously therapeutic. Some trained hospice professionals use recorded memories as a form of therapy.[4] This book is not a guide about how to do that. This is about assisting and honoring your Star. The Star decides what he or she wants to share. Someone who has experienced war may choose not to record those memories or any negative experiences or feelings. Others will talk a great deal about their war experiences and never mention that a first-born child died at the age of two. This is his or her personal record, and he or she alone elects to share what goes into that record.

> An idea that is developed and put into action is more important than an idea that exists only as an idea.
> ~ Buddha

You have several decisions to make regarding the content and format of the Life Reflections video. First, take time to read about our experiences and discover your best path. Review all the sections of this guide carefully so that you can approach this project with confidence. Technology changes every day. But the one thing that does not change is the clock that keeps ticking. Time cannot be stopped.

Don't Wait: Use Existing Equipment

The Encyclopedia Britannica® is no longer available in print as of 2010. "It's a rite of passage in this new era," said Jorge Cauz, the president of Encyclopaedia Britannica Inc. "Some people will feel sad about it and nostalgic about it. But we have a better tool now. The website is continuously updated, it's much more expansive, and it has multimedia."[5] After 2012, Apple computers will not include built-in DVD burners in future models. That technology will be obsolete. It is difficult to keep pace with changing technologies, so our advice is to use what you have available today.

Chances are, even if you don't own a camcorder, you already possess some kind of video recording device. Just think about it: smartphones, iPads, and digital cameras all record video. As you consider the following overview of recording equipment types, pay close attention to the one you currently own. Become familiar with the characteristics of your device and its post-production options. Check your equipment to ensure that it records quality video, has a hookup for an exterior microphone, and has a way to mount on a tripod. It should also have a battery and memory space that accommodates a fifteen- to thirty-minute video.

The consumer camcorder market has dropped off considerably over the past few years. The main reason for this is that while it was once necessary to have a camcorder to capture video, many other devices do it now, from smartphones and tablets to digital still cameras that shoot video. Grab whatever camera you have, and let's get started.

Camcorder

Camcorders, which became popular in the early 1980s, are also known as video recorders or video cameras. Professional videographers and filmmakers use camcorders to produce video segments and films for commercial sale. The devices are also popular with amateur videographers.

The first camcorders recorded in one of two analog formats: VHS and Betamax. Recordings were stored on videotape cassettes and replayed with a videotape cassette recorder (VCR) hooked up to a monitor, typically a TV set. As technology improved, other formats such as S-VHS, 8mm, Hi-8, MiniDV, and high-definition video became available. These formats offered a sharper picture, better color, more hours of recording, and more efficient storage.[6] No other video recording device can rival the storage capacity of a camcorder with a built-in hard drive, which offers much more recording time than even your highest-capacity flash memory card.

Camcorders assure the best audio and video quality for recording a Life Reflections video, but they require one additional step during post-production: file conversion. If you are making an *edited* video, this is easily and automatically taken care of by the computer editing software. If you are creating an *unedited* video, the DVD-burner software will make the conversion automatically. When posting a video to YouTube, files need to be converted to a web-friendly format before uploading. Please refer to Chapter 5: It's a Wrap for more on post-production options.

Many still cameras (digital SLRs) have the capability to shoot high-quality video clips. Their memory cards are easy to access and are available in many different sizes. If you are not going to edit your video, you can simply pop out the memory card and take it to a video conversion service to have a DVD burned.

Smartphone

A smartphone is a cellular telephone with an integrated computer and other features not originally associated with telephones, such as a digital camera capable of taking still photos as well as shooting video. Its operating system allows for web browsing and the ability to run software applications. A full-length motion picture, *Olive*, was made exclusively with a smartphone.[7]

Digital SLR Cameras
SLR stands for "single lens reflex." Users look through a mirrored prism to preview the shot. When the shot is taken, the prism flips up, and the shutter is released. An SLR camera has a removable lens, whereas a point-and-shoot camera has a lens that is part of the camera body and cannot be changed.

Camcorder	Compact/Pocket Camcorder	Smartphone	Still camera with video capabilities
Video Quality			
High	Medium/High	Medium (light dependent)	Medium/High
Audio Quality			
Adequate	Low	Low	Low
Built-in microphones adequate if background noise is minimal. Use external mic if possible.	External mic is recommended.	External mic is recommended.	External mic is recommended.
Recording Duration (power, memory)			
High	Low	Low-Medium	Medium
Most storage capacity with built-in and removable memory. Long-lasting rechargeable batteries and/or AC power cord.	Memory cards available in many sizes. Batteries only.	Music/apps/graphics compete for storage space. iPhone has internal memory only. Android has removable memory. Rechargeable internal batteries and/or AC power cord.	Maximum recording time is twenty-nine minutes. Law dictates that cameras exceeding thirty minutes are classified as camcorders. Rechargeable internal batteries and/or AC power cord.
File Format Flexibility			
High	Low	Low	Low
Create various file formats which must be converted before it can be shared.	Create standard file extensions that are easily shared.	Create standard file extensions that are easily shared.	Create video with AVI, .MOV, .MP4, or .MTS extensions
Cost			
Medium	Low	High	Medium
Consumer camcorders range from $250-1500	$150	Monthly data plan	$250 and higher

Camera Comparison Chart

We like recording with smartphones for the simple reason that they are readily available and easy to set up. External microphones have become available recently, which helps users overcome the poor audio typically associated with video captured on a mobile device. Chapter 4: Audio and Lighting Matters includes a review of these microphones. As with a video camera, you have several options for saving the video. With a smartphone, you can easily upload to Facebook®, the social networking giant, or to a media storage application on your own computer or online.

Today's technology will change in the blink of an eye. Our advice is to use what you have access to *today*. Capture the living essence of your family members before they are gone. *Don't wait* for the perfect technology; use what you have today and preserve your legacy. Here is a review of the today's recording technologies. Which one do you currently have?

Three Basic Approaches to Editing

You can complete this precious project with or without a computer. What we call an "unedited" Life Reflections video transpires when we record an interview more or less nonstop from start to finish and publish the recording "as is." The finished product is a minimally edited video. This first type of Life Reflections video takes more initial planning; however, with forethought, you can produce a streamlined video your family will enjoy.

If you enjoy film editing and have a robust computer, you may want to create a self-edited Life Reflections video. First, explore the basic film editing software that was included with your computer. Other inexpensive editing software is available for Intel and MacIntosh computers. A multimedia Life Reflections video is a fully edited production that might include multiple camera angles, the introduction of music, voice-overs, still photos, graphics, and other special effects. Edited Life Reflections require significantly more post-production time and can take from five to ten times as many hours to complete. One hour of editing can equal about one minute of finished video, depending on your expertise and equipment.

Thirdly, if you want all the bells and whistles of a multimedia Life Reflections video, it might be wise to enlist the services of a professional video production company. It costs more ($500 to $3,000), but the value is immeasurable. So do it yourself, or hire someone else to help—you have the choice.

Video scrapbooks are the wave of the future and will become commonplace in family archiving projects.

Video screenings link generations.

Editing and sharing options have changed drastically with digital cameras. Scenes of your original video can be viewed now or edited later. Your options are limitless. You can send your raw footage to a production house or to a teenage family member, or you can do it yourself. The goal is to capture the priceless memories here and now and figure out how to share it.

Sharing the Video

Determine when and how to share your project. Sharing the video is a very important part of this process; do not take it lightly. You may choose to have a screening party or to share the Life Reflections video at a special event such as a family reunion or through personal road shows with family and friends.

If you choose to have a screening party, give careful thought to the people whom you think should be present, and make the initial screening of the Life Reflections video into a celebration! You might consider relating to the attendees what the experience meant to you and thank your loved one for sharing this intimate glimpse into his or her soul with you. At times, screening parties may not be desired or practical.

Dave was diagnosed with lung cancer earlier in the year, but at the time of the recording, he was energetic and active. He loved the process, and he loved the result. His Life Reflections video was full of optimistic quotes and advice for the youngsters. Dave traveled more than one thousand miles to deliver copies of his Life Reflections DVD to his with brothers, sisters, nephews, and nieces. The process was bittersweet. His daughter, Kim, said it best: "If I ever feel at a loss or off-track, I can play this DVD and remember my Dad's advice for what's important in life."[8]

At Parting Thoughts, after a project is completed, we invite the Star, along with family members and friends, to join us for a

> Because Paul fatigued quickly, we decided to divide the recording into two sessions. However, we were unable to complete the second recording before Paul's condition became grave and ultimately he died. His family was thrilled with the short segment of video footage we had captured. We are reminded over and over again that you cannot predict the future, and you must grasp the opportunity when it is available.

> Take your show on the road! American motion picture road shows were featured films that opened in a limited number of theaters in large cities. The practice had mostly ended by the 1970s.

screening of the Life Reflections video. As the video begins, we often initiate casual banter to lighten the mood of the room. Soon, however, as the loved one's video begins, the room is deeply silent as the audience members realize what they are seeing. These events are, at times, deep and emotional, and no one can speak for a few moments after the screening, only weep—including those of us involved in the creation of the Life Reflections.

Many times, family members are hearing stories that our interviewers gathered for the first time—they are completely captivated, moment by moment, frame by frame. It is usual for a reverent silence to fill the room for the rest of the screening except for the occasional laughter or sniffle. We never screen without numerous boxes of tissues placed strategically throughout the room.

Regardless of the length, quality, or format of your video, anything is better than nothing.

Digital Knight Photography-Doug Havens

The only thing you take with you when you're gone is what you leave behind. –John Allston

Starting Thoughts Review

Your Star

Who is the subject of your video?

_____

Where is your Star located? Can you easily travel to your Star?

_____

Is there an upcoming occasion scheduled at which you will want to share the video (family reunion, birthday, anniversary, etc.)?

_____

What is your Star's current medical condition? Do you need to capture the Life Reflections video this week? This month? This year?

_____

_____

_____

Recording Equipment Evaluation

What recording equipment do you currently have access to?

_____

_____

What are the strengths and limitations of the equipment?

_____

_____

What type of microphone does the recorder have? What special adjustments will need to be made to accommodate this type of microphone? Do you need a special microphone that can pick up a weak voice?

_____

_____

Do you have the owner's manual, and are you comfortable recording with the equipment? Do you need additional training?

_____

_____

Do you have a tripod?

_____

_____

Do you have headphones? Do you know how they attach and interface with camera?

_____

Editing Approach

What is your editing approach (unedited, self-edited, professionally edited)?

_____

_____

How will you share the Life Reflections video? (screening party, road show, online?)

_____

_____

What is the preliminary date for celebration/personal visit?

_____

_____

Who will be invited to the event and/or visited personally? Guest list:

1 _____	6 _____
2 _____	7 _____
3 _____	8 _____
4 _____	9 _____
5 _____	10 _____

If you are having a screening party, what equipment will be used to play the video? A flat-screen TV? A projector? A DVD player?

_____

Chapter Two:

PLANNING OVER A CUP OF TEA

Chapter Two

PLANNING OVER A CUP OF TEA

Find yourself a cup; the teapot is behind you.

Now tell me about hundreds of things.

~Saki

Develop a Pleasant Rapport: No Cameras Allowed

What is the first step? Invite the interviewee to share a cup of tea. This Planning Over a Cup of Tea step allows you to get acquainted with the person you will be videotaping and to survey the setting. Sharing a cup of tea and conversation in a relaxed atmosphere in which life's questions and answers are the topic helps establish mutual respect between an interviewer and an interviewee. Many cultures have created intricate, formal ceremonies around sharing a hot beverage, and the special occasion of planning a Life Reflections video deserves this high honor.

As people enjoy the tea and the conversation, something unexpected occurs. We have found that a relationship enlightenment of sorts occurs. This high-quality moment is the beginning of a very special journey.

Your Star may have proposed the idea for a Life Reflections video, but it is more likely that you are the person who introduced the notion to your loved one. You undoubtedly are very fond of the person you wish to interview, and you want to have a recording of him or her to keep forever and to share with others. Although you may be asking your Star to do this interview for personal reasons, it is important to keep in mind that your interviewee has the last word. As the interviewer, you are his or her advocate. This role is vital, and you must keep the project focused on this fact. Your loved one should enjoy creating the video and not be stressed or feel uncomfortable. The process development itself is a joyful journey, and the journey is as important as the final product.

Establish Trust: The Reluctant Star

Beginning with a low-stress, one-on-one discussion, you can develop the casual rapport and necessary trust to ease the fears of a reluctant Star. Many people are resistant to having their photo or video taken. They may not wish to be recorded on video for a multitude of reasons: "I just don't look good anymore" or "I don't know what to say" or "I'm not feeling well" are common protestations. You might remind them that this experience is only for the family to witness and that they have ultimate control as to when and with whom to share it. This is one of the reasons you must forge a close bond with your Stars. Remind them that this is a special privilege, an opportunity to share their life story for posterity. Trust is vital, and they must trust you to honor their requests. After all, this is their video, and it must be to their liking. It is your responsibility as their advocate to help represent their story in the best possible light.

> The process itself is a joyful journey, and the journey is as important as the final product.

Then, looking me in the eye, she confided in a hushed tone, "I always wanted to be invisible." I listened as she framed her words.

"When the committee came up with the idea of our women doing personal history work, I just gritted my teeth. 'Why should anyone want to share their story?' I thought. Ever since I was a child, I just wanted to be invisible and have no one notice me at all."

She continued. "I reluctantly came tonight, intending to let the words roll off of me, like I always have. But something changed. I realized that I do have a story—I do have a voice. Maybe it's time to stop feeling invisible."[9]

This important message reminds us that it is time for us all to draw upon the wisdom of our experience and find a voice for what matters in our lives. Ask your hesitant Star, "What questions would you have asked your grandparents if they were recording a Life Reflections video?" It is time to make our stories and values count in the world and do something to answer the question "How will I be remembered?"

Your family member is not telling his or her story because of his personal ego; rather, it is at your behest. Gently remind your potential Star that memories will fade over time, and this is a precious gift that he is bequeathing to you and the family, as well as to the family's posterity. Do your very best to make him feel at ease and convey your excitement for the project.

To gain his initial involvement and generate excitement, you might explain that many people have already recorded Life Reflections videos for their families. Ask the Star, "Do you think the families of those who have recorded Life Reflections videos appreciated it? Who do you think will treasure their videos the most? What do you want future generations to know about your own parents and grandparents?" This is a delicate conversation. It will encourage him to think of the benefits for not only himself but also for his family. The answer to this important question of motivation will be the first item addressed in the Life Reflections video.

Have complete confidence in yourself, and make sure your loved one understands how important preserving his life story is to you. This is a priceless gift for all of you—and it may change your lives because of the deepened relationships and the stories revealed.

Define Story Topics and Supporting "Anchor Points"

A Life Reflections video is real-life commentary that will enliven existing journals and scrapbooks. We call these videos life "reflections," not life "reviews," because they reflect important life moments or lessons. The Life Reflections video is not intended to chronicle someone's entire life. It is not a mini-series. The intention is to capture, on video, a sense of the person: his or her passions and the things he or she holds dear. Planning Over a Cup of Tea is your chance to learn about and outline your family member's wishes for the video's focus. Your finished video should be fifteen to thirty minutes long. Therefore, it will include only a few carefully chosen topics. We suggest no more than three. To support each topic, provide examples that "anchor" the story to the topic. We refer to these examples as "anchor points." The topic of cooking might be anchored with favorite recipes and memories of cooking Thanksgiving dinner. Anchor points give structure to the topic outline and enable the interviewer to keep the interview on course. If you intend to post your video online, these distinct topic sections are good markers for dividing the video into short, web-friendly segments. We suggest that you complete the Topic and Anchor Point Chart included at the

Why Make a Life Reflections Video?

• "So my grandchildren and future grandchildren can see what the life of crazy Nana was like. I wanted them to know that their Nana was not always old."

• "So my grandchildren and great-grandchildren will understand how good they have it today!"

• "So that after I'm gone, they will know more of our family history."

end of this chapter. Review the following example of a completed chart illustrating the topic "Loving Relationships" with corresponding anchor points, interview prompts, and potential visual supports.

Topic	Anchor Points	Interview Prompts and Supporting Photos and/or Memorabilia
Introduction	Ask Star to state date and name (spell name). State why you are making a Life Reflections video.	Ask this question first before you press "record" on the camera. Then nod to the Star to signal that he should begin.
Topic #1: 60-year marriage	Anchor point #1a: Respect others' space	Prompt: "What are the secrets to a successful marriage?" Show wedding photo.
	Anchor Point #1b: Fight fair	Prompt: "Tell me about your marriage." Show wedding ring.
Topic #2	Anchor Point #2a	
	Anchor Point #2b	
	Anchor Point #2c	

Topic and Anchor point chart example

As the interviewer, determine the topic(s) of the Life Reflections video and anchor each topic with several specific anecdotes that support the points within the topic. Photos and photo albums, written correspondence, and war medals or awards can help guide the topic-selection process. All of these treasured artifacts are wonderful and can provide the foundation for introducing the anecdotes of your family member. Ask your Star if he would like to share a few photographs and/or memorabilia to show on camera during the Armchair Interview. If you are making an unedited Life Reflections video, this is the only way to include these treasures because you will not have the option to add scanned photos later. These items are also useful to "get the ball rolling" during recording. Guide your Star through the subject-matter selection as you complete the Topic and Anchor Point Chart together.

Video Topic Ideas:

✓ Childhood

✓ Church

✓ Recipes

✓ Love

✓ Family lore

✓ Musical talent

✓ Life lessons

Video topics are personal and represent a diverse range of experiences and emotions. These may include ruminations and advice about the importance of loving relationships and can be presented as a gift to a recently wed grandchild. The topic would be "loving relationships," and the anchor points might include "respecting each other's space, fighting fair, and making time for each other." Another topic might address the importance of patriotism and freedom and include personal war experiences as anchor points within that topic.

Some people discuss only the happiest times of their lives such as vacations, adventures, and their children's births and accomplishments. We created a video in which one woman focused solely on her religion and her activities in the various groups within her church. It was critical to her that she leave a testimony of her faith. In another Life Reflections video, a man presented a lesson on effective parenting and the meaning and importance of love in a parent/child relationship. Sometimes, deep secrets are revealed. One woman spoke of her devastation when her first husband left her for another woman, and then, in heartbreaking detail never before shared with her daughters, she told the story of her eventual solace and great joy when she finally met the "other woman's" cuckolded husband—who went on to become the love of her life and her second husband. This joyful journey of disclosure can begin a healing process. One man who had been estranged from his family for years became reacquainted with his family as he reflected on past mistakes. He made amends, enabling all of them to move toward reconciliation.

As you progress with the project, you will continue to feel an abundance of love, compassion, and understanding. For a person nearing the end of life, it is precious beyond words. At the conclusion of the recording, your special person may feel emotionally exhausted. Many of our clients report that they sleep exceptionally late the morning following their recording session—but awaken with the satisfaction of a job well done.

The interviewer's role is to lead the interviewee down the path charted by the anchor points. The trick is to focus the interview on no more than three topic segments so that the project does not become overwhelming. If you try to do a review of an entire life, the recording can result in a frustrating search for dates, correct spellings, and accuracy. Keep in mind that those details are usually captured in the family's scrapbooks and journals. Your focus with a Life Reflections video is to let the Star shine. Some people are quite adept at recalling details, while others are not. Often, the struggle to recall certain details can distract from the goal of the joyful journey.

Assess the Setting: Note Video and Audio Concerns

The backdrop to your video heirloom reveals much about your Star's life and curent lifestyle. We recommend that you seat your Star in the most comfortable and stable chair. Often this is a favorite recliner or reading chair. It is important to brace the chair firmly so it does not move during the interview; the natural inclination to rock will become an annoying distraction on the video. The familiarity of this well-known environment will diminish apprehension and promote a more relaxed dialogue.

If your loved one is confined to bed, this setting will need additional scrutiny. Evaluate this situation with regard to preserving the person's dignity, and try to minimize the sterility of the setting. Consider exchanging plain white pillowcases for a floral pattern or a warm color to evoke a more cheery, home-like feel. You may also want to add a framed photograph (possibly a picture of him or her as a young person), flowers, or other attractive accessories on a nearby table. Remember to place a small, easy-to-grasp glass of water within reach. If recording in a medical setting, consider bringing a small, colorful glass to replace the sterile plastic cups used in most health care environments.

Identify Unwanted Noise Culprits

Take time to look around. Do you *see* any sources of undesirable noise? Close your eyes and listen. Do you *hear* any extraneous noise? Identify the culprits on the Noise Surveillance Evaluation worksheet and make a plan to eliminate or reduce them on recording day. It is common for interviews to take place in the living room

Just as Norma was beginning to share a great anecdote about her father, we heard "scratch, scratch, scratch." And then, "whimper, whimper, whimper." Her dogs wanted inside. Norma kept talking without missing a beat. Despite editing, many of the scratches and whimpers were audible in the finished video. Everyone agreed that the unplanned dog "sound effects" did add a certain character and truth to the video. It truly was her story—her way.

of a home. These rooms are not quiet, and microphones built into your camera will tend to amplify any background noise. For example, a battery-operated wall clock may sound like a ticking time bomb with this type of microphone. We have shot video where a remote laundry washing machine operating in another part of the house went undetected during recording, only becoming evident when we began editing the Life Reflections video. We were dismayed.

Due to these audio challenges, as well as the possibly diminished voice strength of your Star, you may want to use an external microphone, as we will explain in Chapter 4: Audio and Video Matters. Now is the time to fill in the first two sections of the Noise Surveillance Evaluation worksheet. Complete the status section of this worksheet on the day you record the video. Solutions to many intrusive sounds are included in this worksheet example. Add other noises you find during your own noise surveillance assessment.

Outside Noises

You have no control over many outside noises such as traffic and neighbors, so let us review just the things you may be able to change or alter. Look out the window. Is there an air conditioner compressor nearby? Are wind chimes ringing in the breeze? Perhaps you can take these down for an hour or immobilize them with tape or an elastic band. If a neighbor's noise could possibly ruin the session (such as a someone in an assisted-care facility with a blaring television), politely ask them to eliminate all disturbances until the session is finished. Just explain to them what you are doing, and surely they will comply.

Inside Noises

Electronics and Appliances: A television, even if located in an adjoining room, may generate ambient noise. Try not to schedule the recording interview during the Star's favorite TV program because he or she may be distracted, knowing that he or she is missing a favorite show. If you must schedule at such a time, recommend taping the show on a DVR or DVD or have a friend tape it for them. Keep computers far away from the microphone. A computer has a fan that sporadically might make a lot of noise to keep the computer motor cooled. Mute any automatic alerts that may occur on phones, computers, or other devices. See if you can turn cooling/heating systems and ceiling fans off. Sounds from nearby rooms such as laughter, a television, and music should be addressed.

Phones: Turn off or unplug household phones. Shut down cell phones and texting devices. These devices must be *off*, not just muted or silenced, because the frequency will cause a hum in the microphones.

Pets: Pets should not be in the room during the interview, even cats with contented purring. Francis Ford Coppola relates that while shooting the movie *The Godfather*, a cat jumped up onto Marlon Brando's lap. Brando began to pet the cat, and without anyone realizing it at the time of filming, the cat's purring was distinctly recorded on audio. Coppola left this unplanned noise in his movie, but you may not feel similarly benevolent about your Star's dog barking at an unexpected FedEx delivery in the middle of an emotional tale.

Other: We have experienced squawking birds, dogs that noisily jumped at a closed door, and cats that continued to leap on and off the focal person's lap during the interview. At one shoot, a cat in heat literally knocked our camera aside with her antics! Our advice is to be aware of the potential distractions and do what you can to minimize their impact.

> The meowing cat problem: Berta's cat was in heat and in the room. Moving the cat did not relieve the cat's meow. It was quieter to actually have the cat in the room. We ended the video with a picture of the cat meowing. If you can't change it—embrace it!

Manage Special Audio Circumstances

If you have background noise, sometimes you have to embrace it (or pet it). For example, if the sound of a waterfall is present in the recording, and the waterfall is visible in the background, the viewer can more easily tune out the distracting sound.

Perhaps soothing background music will help to mask any unexpected or uncontrollable noises. If your Star has some favorite classical music pieces you can play these softly from behind the chair to both mask noise and soothe the Star. This is an especially easy way to add music to an unedited Life Refections video, as long as you ensure that the music does not compete with the volume of the Star's voice on your recording.

On-Set Noises: We suggest using memory-prompting photographs because they are wonderful interviewing tools. Take care to avoid paper noises: shuffling, dropping, crinkling, etc. Likewise, interviewers should be vigilant to keep their own notes out of camera view and to slide, rather than flip, notes.

Oxygen: Some subjects may be using oxygen concentrators, of which there are various types. Some have nostril tubes, while others may have a mask that covers the nose and mouth. Nose-clamp models present the least amount of challenge for the videographer. Clients can keep it in during the interview with little adverse effect on the finished product. We have never done an interview with a person who could not remove the mask for short periods of time. In situations like these, we pause regularly to give him or her plenty of time to rest with the oxygen mask on before proceeding with other sections of the interview. Floor-model oxygen concentrators tend to be louder than other models. If possible, switch to a portable concentrator, and locate it away from and behind the microphones. Moving the concentrator completely out of the room is best. Never record in a manner that violates medical recommendations, and always take care to make sure the Star is safe and comfortable.

Motorized Beds: Even when adjustable electric beds are idle, many models emit a constant low-frequency hum. It is best to position the bed properly as you set up the shoot, and then, after the bed is placed, ask permission to unplug the bed for the duration of the recording.

Madeleine had a very soft voice; therefore, we selected an external lavalier microphone. Her cat, Jazzy, showed up several times during taping. We weren't concerned with that because Jazzy added a nice touch to Madeleine's Life Reflections video. However, we learned later that each time the cat jumped onto Madeleine's lap, she brushed against our lavalier microphone cable, creating a loud audio click. Now, whenever animals are going to be present and we're using external mics, we secure cables where they're least likely to be bumped by friends like Jazzy.

Outside Noises	Solution	Status (complete on recording day)
Door bell	Place tape over the button and post a "Do Not Disturb" sign.	
Barking neighborhood dogs	Alert neighbors about the scheduled recording.	
Central air conditioning condenser	Turn off during taping.	

Traffic	Schedule interview during quietest time of day.	
Wind chimes	Remove the chimes or tape them together.	
Inside Noises	**Solution**	**Status**
Household phone	Power off or unplug.	
Cell phone	Power off (do not mute).	
Alarm	Disable schedule alarms (alarm clocks, computer alerts, wrist watches).	
Ceiling fan	Turn off.	
Clock	Remove batteries/relocate	
Tabletop or floor fan	Turn off	
Computer	Unplug or relocate to a different room.	
Electric bed	Turn off power.	
Dishwasher	Turn off for duration of recording.	
Furnace	Turn off for duration of recording.	

Noise surveillance evaluation example

Is Now a Good Time? Scheduling Considerations

Establish a time and date for the recording session. Choose the best period of day for both of you, when you will be uninterrupted and can focus solely on the interview. For example, if Grandma or Grandpa tires easily in the afternoon, set a morning appointment. Allow enough time to set up the camera, address lighting and extraneous noisemakers, and ease into the recording task. Typically, the entire set-up and recording process takes two to three hours.

Coordinate with neighbors, nurses, facility staff, and other service providers to reserve a block of time that ensures an uninterrupted recording session. Post a "Recording in Progress" sign on the door. In assisted-care facilities, it is common for intercom announcements to blare out without notice. While the facility may not discontinue these announcements, you can ask managers when they typically occur and plan accordingly. They may even agree to discontinue announcements during the recording session after you have explained the situation.

Designate and communicate to others a precise block of time when the room (and preferably the entire house) is as quiet as technically possible. Discuss the schedule with the family and any staff, if applicable, and note the times of day that tend to be the most quiet and have fewer intrusive outside noises.

> Assisted-living facilities have predictable, routine procedures, including mealtime intercom announcements and medical staff who make room visits. Before scheduling shooting times in a residential or assisted-living center, we always talk to management.

Not-So-Innocent Bystanders: Audience Rules

Carefully consider whether to allow extras on the set. We have found that family and well-intentioned friends can very often create a layer of stress that is unnecessary. Well-loved stories may have been told so often that others like to jump in or correct the Star if something in the story seems to have been left out or not told in the most diplomatic way. This is supposed to be a fun and perhaps even cathartic experience for your loved one, and everyone must keep in mind that this entire experience, from the telling of the story to the final product of the video, is for the benefit of your loved one. He or she is the center of attention, and no one else.

If extras are included, please post the following rules:

> **Audience Rules:**
>
> ✓ No talking to the main
>   attraction or to each other
> ✓ No phone calls
> ✓ No texting or computer use
> ✓ No cleaning
> ✓ No cooking
> ✓ No eating
> ✓ No chewing gum

Star Appearance

Your Star needs to feel confident and prepared. How your loved one feels about himself or herself will be reflected in the video. It is a good idea to give consideration to clothing, makeup, and hair.

Clothing: Make sure that the furniture and your Star's clothing do not have odd colors or clashing patterns. A good rule of thumb: patterned chair—solid shirt. Patterned shirt—solid chair. Also make sure the colors are a complementary color pairing.

Makeup: Aging skin tends to become pale and may develop age spots. At Parting Thoughts, we typically do not recommend makeup beyond what our patrons normally wear. We may use a bit of concealing makeup to touch up blemishes and apply a splash of color on cheeks and lips before shooting begins.

Hair: A haircut or hairstyle will not only make the Star look good; it will make him or her feel better, too. There is nothing like a new haircut to make one feel happier and more refreshed.

After completing Chapter 2: Planning Over a Cup of Tea, you should have a good idea of how the recording process will go. Hopefully, you have established a warm rapport with your Star, understand the motivation for the video, have outlined the topics, and have addressed the site and appearance considerations.

To-Do's:

- Complete the Topic and Anchor Point Chart.

- Complete the Noise Surveillance Evaluation Worksheet ("Potential Noises" and "Solutions" sections).

- Complete the Setting and Star Appearance Worksheet.

- Ask the Star to collect desired photos and/or memorabilia to show during recording (especially important if creating an unedited video).

- Schedule the Armchair Interview.

Topic and Anchor Point Chart

Topic	Anchor Points	Interview Prompts and supporting Photos and/or Memorabilia
	Ask Star to state: — Date — Name and spelling — Reason he/she is making a Life Reflections video	Review the "introduction" with your Star. Start background music if desired, especially if creating an unedited video. Press the videocamera's "record" button and give a nod to your Star to begin speaking
Topic #1	Anchor Point #1a	
	Anchor Point #1b	

LIFE REFLECTIONS

Topic	Anchor Points	Interview Prompts and supporting Photos and/or Memorabilia
	Anchor Point #1c	
Topic #2	Anchor Point #2a	
	Anchor Point #2b	

Topic	Anchor Points	Interview Prompts and supporting Photos and/or Memorabilia
	Anchor Point #2c	
Topic #3	Anchor Point #3a	
	Anchor Point #3b	
	Anchor Point #3c	

Setting and Star Appearance Worksheet

Setting

Is the designated chair solid? Does is creak or rock? What is the chair color?

_____

Have you placed personal artifacts on the side table such as framed photographs or flowers ?   Will items need to be removed or added?

_____

What extraneous noises are detected? Use the Noise Surveillance Evaluation Worksheet to identify and report the status of noises.

_____

Appearance

Make barber/stylist appointment if desired.

Date/Time _____

Wardrobe Choices (complement and contrast to chair)

Shirt/blouse _____

Trousers/skirt _____

Dress _____

Noise Surveillance Evaluation Worksheet

Use this template to record the potentially distracting sounds you observe in your individual setting. Refer to this list on the recording day to complete the status section.

Outside Noises

Potential Noises	Solution	Status (complete on recording day)
Door bell	Place tape over the button. Post "Do Not Disturb Sign" on front door	✓ ✓

Noise Surveillance Evaluation Worksheet

Inside Noises

Potential Noises	Solution	Status
Household Phone	Turn off or unplug	✓
Cell Phones	Turn power off (dont just silence)	✓

SIGN TO POST ON THE SET

Audience Rules:

— No talking to the interviewee or to each other

— No phone calls

— No texting or computer use

— No cleaning

— No cooking

— No eating

— No chewing gum

Chapter Three:

THE ARMCHAIR INTERVIEW

Chapter Three

THE ARMCHAIR INTERVIEW

Tell me a fact and I'll learn. Tell me a truth and I'll believe. But tell

me a story and it will live in my heart forever.

~Indian Proverb

Provide Quiet Support

Planning Over a Cup of Tea has prepared you and the Star for this big day. Excitement is in the air. Relax and, whatever you do, have fun! Despite the distracting equipment, this is really just a conversation between you and your family member. However, keep in mind that it's a conversation in which you, as the interviewer, will do more listening than speaking. Your role in the Armchair Interview process is one of support— non-verbal, engaged, encouraging.

As the interviewer, do more listening than speaking.

Some people might feel a bit self-conscious when sitting down to begin the interview. The recording equipment may be intimidating, but if you create a friendly, comfortable, and welcoming environment for your subject, all of the equipment will seem to fade into the background. You and your subject will be having too much fun to focus on anything except your conversation.

Whether you are planning an unedited, self-edited, or professionally edited video, your goal should be to create as clean an interview as possible, thereby reducing the necessity to edit mistakes in post-production.

As the interviewer, your goal is to get your subject to reminisce about the chosen topics without any verbal cues from you. Before pressing the record button on the videocamera review the Topic and Anchor Point Chart together. As you review remind your Star to avoid a mere recitation of facts.

Your role in the interview process is one of support— nonverbal, engaged, encouraging.

When speaking to a skilled interviewer in a relaxed setting, invariably half-forgotten memories and richer stories emerge. The Star's character comes shining through in his or her manner of speech, humor, and perceptions.

Be present to the person. Show that you understand and appreciate what he or she is talking about. If you did not hear something or don't understand a concept, ask for clarification. Laughing is fine, but be silent with *your* laughter. Explain to the interviewee that you want to capture only the sound of his or her voice on the video.

If an interruption occurs while taping, or the Star needs a break, the classic gesture of making a "stop" or "cut" motion across your throat will work. Everyone in the room will need to communicate in this way so that the audio portion of the video remains free of unnecessary and distracting chatter. The fewer people in the recording area, the better your taping will go. On Hollywood movie sets, "extras" may be desirable at times, but they are not wanted during the filming of love scenes, for example. This intimate Life Reflections recording needs the same sensitivity and privacy as a love scene.

Ideally, your communication during the interview will be nonverbal. Smiling, constant eye contact, leaning forward, nodding, and using hand gestures are all nonverbal tools you will use during the interview. With the camera lens in such close proximity to your own head, your eye contact is vital to maintaining the interviewee's connection to the camera.

Proper preparation is the key to an outstanding interview. Arrive on-site with all of your equipment carefully checked and all batteries fully charged and your chosen video-editing path in mind. Please review the Day of Interview Checklist included in this chapter to allow your Star to shine.

Set the Stage

Allow plenty of time to set the stage for the Armchair Interview. You may need to move furniture to take advantage of natural light and to position the camera and tripod for the most flattering camera angle. We suggest that you establish one flattering camera angle and leave it for the duration of the interview. If you need to get closer to your subject, follow the old photographer's maxim: Zoom with your feet. Locate the camera and interviewer's chair about three to five feet away from the Star to eliminate the need to zoom excessively. Do not zoom in or alter framing during the interview because future viewers may find that movement distracting. Advise the Star to use this set-up time to collect his or her own thoughts "off-stage."

> Ensure that your camera angle flatters your subject! Avoid highlighting double chins.

Equipment Set-Up

You can purchase a videographer's vital tool, a tripod, inexpensively. The tripod provides stability and ensures that the most flattering framing of your subject will be maintained throughout the interview. Don't forget to pack the tripod's camera plate, as they are small and easily misplaced.

The size of the room and the room layout will ultimately dictate your camera set-up. Place your camera in a location that allows for comfortable conversation. Proper framing of your shot is essential and surprisingly simple. You, the interviewer, will sit next to the camera, which will result in the Star directing his or her comments toward you and therefore toward the camera, too. This naturally results in an attractive camera perspective. The camera angle should be approximately at eye level or slightly higher to ensure the most flattering shot. Look for unsightly shadows under noses and eyes or highlighted double chins, and correct the lighting and/or camera angle as needed. Remind the Star to maintain eye contact with you, and only you, throughout the interview.

> The life review, as sometimes manifested by nostalgia and reminiscence, is a natural healing process. Some of the positive results of a life review can be the righting of old wrongs, making up with estranged family members or friends, coming to accept one's mortality, gaining a sense of serenity, pride in accomplishment, and a feeling of having done one's best.[10]
>
> ~K. J. Doka

Check the framing within the video camera viewfinder. Allow room in the viewfinder for arm and hand movements to show on the screen. Ensure that personal items such as prescription bottles, tissue boxes, and dishes are not visible. If you are shooting where medical equipment is present, try to minimize its appearance in the video. For example, you can lower bed rails out of the shot.

Remove Distractions and Noises

Use the completed Noise Surveillance Evaluation (Chapter 2: Planning Over a Cup of Tea) to make the needed adjustments to inside and outside distractions and noises. We cannot reiterate enough how important it is to remove all potential distractions from the recording area, including family members and pets. Phones should be turned off and clocks relocated to a room where they cannot possibly be heard. Put tape over any doorbells and a large note on the door that says Do Not Disturb! Recording in Progress.

On-Camera Editing:

1. Stop.
2. Rerecord.
3. Trim.

Assure that you have removed background noise and that your Star can be heard clearly by recording a final check of your what your camera is actually seeing and hearing. You can conduct a sample test by recording and then playing back for a few minutes. This will allow you to assess the audio and video quality.

Check the audio settings before you start the video recording to make sure that your Star can be heard clearly, and listen for unwanted background noises. Do some testing on-site before and after seating your Star. "Check: One, two, three!" By using headphones plugged into your recording device, you will hear details that go unnoticed without headphones. It is similar to the effect of using the zoom lens on your camera, which reveals information unnoticed from a distance. You can use headphones that you already have for your stereo/iPod or rent them at an audio store. When you listen to the audio through headphones, you will hear exactly what the camera is recording—which is a good thing. You may add musical elements to your video recording by playing a favorite song during part of the recording. It is wiser to play an instrumental selection such as soft guitar and cello, which is easier to talk through when the volume is set low. Have the musical selection ready to turn on before you start recording.

Tips for an Unedited Video

If you will not edit the video recording by downloading to a computer, you can still alter the recording by turning the camera on and off as you record and trimming the movie files after your interview is completed. "Trimming" the ends of each video file is accomplished as the recording is played back on your camera or smartphone. Be sure to familarize yourself with your equipment or consult the camera's manual. Use your hand signals to stop the recording due to distractions or if your focus person decides that he or she wants to edit or retell part of the story just told. Stop the recording promptly after a mistake is made. This will allow you to later edit the unwanted "end" of any video file on your Smartphone or camcorder. With unedited videos, we suggest that you record in segments of approximately ten minutes in order to create multiple, manageable files. These files can be transferred to a DVD sequentially or easily shared individually to websites like Facebook or YouTube. "Trim" the movie file(s) only after you have finished recording the entire interview in order to maintain the momentum and flow of the interview.

©www.harrycutting.com

Include old photos in your unedited video by displaying them for the camera.

Do not be afraid of mistakes in the process. If something is forgotten or not explained exactly as one wishes, you can either stop and re-record the story, or just enjoy the story as initially explained. You are capturing a slice of your loved one's life, and that life may include dogs barking or cats sitting on laps. So be it.

You can add historical images to the video recording by having your special person hold up old photographs for the camera while they talk about the subjects in the photo. In fact, holding up a treasured photo or object stimulates conversations, facial expressions, and hand gestures.

A great way to make the video exciting is to have the Star speak while shooting each photograph individually. Simply ask the Star to hold one of the photographs toward the camera, then direct the camera lens toward the photograph for at least five seconds. Your grandfather's old war photos or your aunt's heirloom tea set might tell us just as much as words can. When you're shooting a Life Reflections video, it is always a good idea to include objects that reveal the rest of the story.

Remember: this interview should be fun for everyone, especially the family and the loved one. An abundance of research is
available that evaluates the wonderful impact that reminiscing has
on the quality of life for older people. Depending on your relationship with the interviewee, his or her oft-told stories might become
a new and fresh version during the interview. It is widely said that
the best gift you can give to another is the gift of listening. You are
about to see for yourself what a gift you will be receiving as well
as giving.

Action! Begin the Interview

Your Star can now take a seat. Take a few minutes to review
the Topics and Anchor Point Chart together. Remember that you
are the Star's advocate. Monitor his or her appearance at all times.
Stay attuned to any nervousness before the interview starts, and
try to help alleviate it. You can do this with a joke, an encouraging
smile, and a compliment on the interviewee's appearance. Many older people have dry mouths and
salivary dysfunction. Keep a tissue handy for them to swab their lips if needed. Women might want to
reapply their lipstick periodically.

> Miriam's two beloved daughters frequently interrupted her story to "correct" the details. There was a lot of starting, stopping, and restarting while the three tried to reach agreement on how the story would turn out.

Turn on the camera. Once the camera starts rolling, do a one- or two-minute test recording. Double-
check the video recording to make sure that the color and sound quality are good. Rewind, play, and
assess. Once you are happy with the way your camera is capturing your subject, you will start your
Armchair Interview. Occasionally, check to make sure that the camera's counter is increasing so that
you do not miss any of the interview.

Your very first topic will be the introduction. Ask your Star to state his or her full name and the
date and to articulate why he or she wants to make the video. People have myriad reasons for desiring
to leave their personal video messages, and it is a good idea for the interviewer to have those thoughts
in mind throughout the interview.

You have reviewed the topics and anchor points with your special person, so all you have to do is
gently guide the interview with minimal interruptions, making sure to cover them all. You and the Star
may have already decided to have him or her share several pictures or pieces of memorabilia during
the recording, so make sure those items are easily accessible from the armchair.

Certain approaches to the beginning of any interviews should be consistent with every recording.
Maintaining eye contact is essential and enhances your interaction with the interviewee. Stay focused

on your subject. Smile along with him or her. Nod your head. The more engaged you are, the more comfortable your subject will feel.

Another essential ingredient to the interview is listening. The subject has a great deal to say. Watching you write notes instead of listening intently will make him or her uncomfortable. The dialogue will drag and become stilted. Soon the subject's interest may disappear. Do not tire out your Star. If your loved one appears fatigued, ask if he or she needs a break. If so, take a breather. Listen with your eyes, ears, and heart.

To-Do's:

- Complete the Day Before Interview Checklist.

- Complete the Day of Interview Checklist.

Blooper: One of our Stars, a gentleman, chose to wear shorts for his interview. It was awkward because we had to rearrange his shorts to a more modest position several times throughout the interview.

Day Before Interview Checklist

Things to Do

☐ Confirm the interview time with the Star.

☐ Check your equipment:
  - Charge the camera battery.
  - Clean the camera lens.
  - Check the microphone
  - Select any music to be used during the interview (e.g., CD, iPod playlist).

☐ Review Worksheets:
  - Noise Surveillance Evaluation Worksheet
  - Day of Interview Checklist
  - Topic and Anchor Point Chart

Things to Pack

☐ Equipment:
  - Camera tripod
  - Camera plate for tripod
  - Microphone
  - Headphones
  - Extension cord/batteries
  - Music player to be used during the interview (e.g., CD player, iPod)

☐ Miscellaneous items:
  - Attractive cup/glass if needed
  - Masking and duct tape
  - "Do Not Disturb" sign
  - Large-watt light bulbs to increase lighting
  - Makeup (blemish concealer)
  - Framed photo of Star for side table
  - Colorful pillowcase or throw

☐   Completed Worksheets:
- Day of Interview Checklist
- Topic and Anchor Point Chart
- Noise Surveillance Evaluation Worksheet

Day of Interview Checklist

☐ Hang a "Do Not Disturb" sign on the exterior door(s).

☐ Post an "Audience Rules" sign and review it with any extras on the set.

☐ Set the stage (add flowers and/or a photo, remove medical stuff, etc.).

☐ Test and set up equipment: Set up tripod, conduct video framing, check audio quality, adjust lighting adjustments, cue music to be played (if any).

☐ Review and resolve the noise issues listed on the Noise Surveillance Evaluation Worksheet.

☐ Review the completed Topic and Anchor Point Chart with the Star. Compile supporting photos or memorabilia and determine sequence.

☐ Review the non-verbal interview signal for "stop," such as a hand crossing in front of the throat.

☐ Place a glass of water nearby.

☐ Monitor the Star's appearance throughout the recording.

☐ Relax and smile!

Chapter Four:

AUDIO AND LIGHTING MATTERS

Chapter Four

AUDIO AND LIGHTING MATTERS

Ring the bells that still can ring. Forget your perfect offering.

There is a crack in everything. That's how the light gets in.

~Leonard Cohen[11]

When planning your video shoot as an amateur, it is best to keep everything simple. This is especially true for filming your interviews. "Simple" means bringing in minimal lights, sound modifiers, and other accessories so that you will not have to spend much of your limited time setting up your equipment.

With that in mind, bring just enough equipment to the set to get the lighting and sound right and just enough experience to deal with the unexpected. Be prepared and stay as flexible as possible. If you are rushed and unprepared, you may stress yourself and then stress your interviewee, which will reflect in your interviews. If, on the other hand, you are confident, relaxed, and good-natured, everybody's job will be easier, and your video recording will be a joy to watch.

Choose the Right Microphone

The importance of a good audio recording on your video cannot be overstated. Remember that you are preparing a visual and audio "feast" for future generations. The setting of the interview has been addressed, and your Star is eager and prepared. However, all of these efforts will be for naught if no one can hear what your Star has to say.

Whether you are using a built-in microphone or another type, always check the audio and video quality using headphones. It is better to know that you are have a problem while still on the set, when the issues can be addressed, than to try to fix it after the shoot, while you are at home watching and possibly editing the video.

Only the Star's voice should be on the recording, so we recommend that the interviewer does not have a separate microphone. Interviewers should use facial expressions for encouragement but should limit comments, questions, and laughter. This is often hard to do because you may want to help the Star along. If you feel a need to provide encouragement, pause the camera, take a break, and begin again.

As you evaluate the microphone options, remember that capturing your Star's voice (not the interviewer's) is your only goal. Older individuals' voices are often softer and quieter than younger people's voices. As we age, we not only become weaker in our arms and legs, but we experience the weakening of the vocal-cord muscles. A hoarse, breathy voice and swallowing problems are common among the elderly. The possibly weaker voice of your loved one makes the reduction and elimination of extraneous audio distractions of utmost importance.

Assess the equipment you already own or have access to. If you need additional equipment, consider renting it. The option of renting microphones from an audio specialty store is especially practicable. The salespeople can help you with the basics you will need to capture quality audio. The rental fee usually ranges from fifty to one hundred dollars per day.

Internal (Built-In) Microphone

Consumer camcorders may not record perfectly crisp audio, but the built-in mics on most models are far better than what you'll find on a smartphone, compact camcorder, or still camera with video capabilities.

We recommend using an external microphone system, but we also recognize that sometimes the internal microphone is your only choice.

The four tiny holes are the internal microphone.

The four little holes on the camera in the picture are the camera's built-in microphone. Most camcorders also have a handy internal microphone. Using the internal microphone is the easiest way to capture the audio for your interview. For the best audio, keep the cameras as close as possible to the Star. It might be tempting to use the camera lens to zoom in for a visual close-up, but the camera must be very close to the subject because the microphone is attached to it. This can be intimidating and uncomfortable for the subject.

The biggest drawback of the internal mic is that it picks up sound from every direction so that you can clearly hear everything outside of your intended frame. Because of this, it is extremely important that everyone on the set is quiet. Extraneous noises will be louder on your recording. If a refrigerator makes a humming noise or an icemaker clunks periodically, the audio system will pick it up. The extraneous noise factor is the main reason we recommend you stay away from using the internal microphone on your camera whenever possible and use an external microphone instead. Remember that, if you are the interviewer, any sounds you make will be especially loud due to your close proximity to the microphone in the camera. Your laughter at an anecdote, for example, will boom compared to your Star's voice. Some camcorders have lens caps that attach to the camera so that the cap won't get lost. If it is swinging and hitting the camera, the internal mic will pick it up. Remove the cap from the camera.

Although we believe you should strongly consider adding a microphone to your camera, we have successfully completed several Life Reflections videos with the on-camera mic. We know that you can produce an acceptable recording using only the internal microphone. We have our own mantra for capturing life's special moments with recording devices: *Memories Fade—Do not wait*. Do not let the absence of an external microphone stop you from capturing a memory.

Joan spontaneously decided to play for us one of her favorite songs on the piano, which was on the opposite side of the room. We swiveled our camera and zoomed in but failed to consider the extra distance between the camera microphone and the piano. Because we were using the on-board mic, we didn't pick up her gentle playing as well we would have liked. We learned an important lesson: Be aware that while the zoom feature on your camera allows you visual close-ups, the audio does not zoom. You are still recording sound with the internal microphone. If you need to change positions, take a few minutes to reposition the camera to ensure great audio as well as great video.

External Microphone

An inexpensive video camera with an inexpensive external mic will outperform a better camera with an internal mic in a room with ambient noise. Most viewers will tolerate a jittery visual shot but will "tune out" if the words are difficult to discern or if the words lag a few seconds after the mouth moves, as in old movies.

Microphones are a good investment because, unlike video cameras, they do not change much over time. A good microphone from fifteen years ago is still an excellent instrument today. You can buy lavalier microphones (the ones that clip on your Star's lapel) for around $30; professional lavaliers can cost $250 and up. A decent shotgun microphone will cost anywhere from $150 to several thousand dollars.[12] The best way to compare prices is to search online, where hundreds of businesses are eager for your purchase. Here is a review of our research on external microphones.

Shotgun Microphone

Shotgun microphones are the most highly directional. They have small lobes of sensitivity to the left, right, and rear that pick up sound but are significantly less sensitive to the side and rear than other directional microphones.

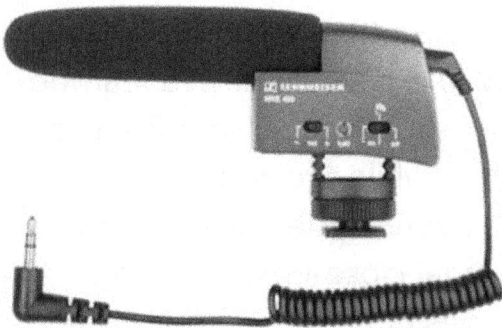

Shotgun Microphone

Shotgun microphones give the subject more flexibility in movement, and Stars do not feel constrained by the cord. Also, these mics are less invasive than attaching a lapel microphone to your Star. A shotgun mic is uni-directional; therefore, the first step to using this mic is to point it directly toward the subject. The closer you get, the better the audio recording. We have placed a shotgun mic on a coffee table, a side table, on the floor, and on a stand. Do your best to keep the microphone out of the visual shot.

Camera-Mounted Microphone

A camera-mounted video microphone may give better sound quality than the built-in microphone, and it will be directional (picking up more of the sound from the direction the camera is pointed toward while eliminating (or at least greatly reducing) other sound. The downside of using this kind of microphone is that you must be close to the subject to get a clear sound.

Camera-mounted microphones for camcorder and DSLR camera

Lavalier (Lapel) Microphone

Lavalier microphone

A lavalier is a pendant with one stone suspended from a necklace. The origin of the term goes back to the type of jewelry pendant popularized by the Duchesse de la Valliere, a mistress of King Louis XIV. Within the fashion world, the name was eventually changed from "Valliere" to "lavalier."[13]

Lavaliers are small microphones that allow hands-free operation. They have small clips for attaching to collars, ties, or other clothing. Always ask for permission before you help a Star attach the lavalier. Experiment with the placement on the shirt. The audio quality and volume varies depending on where you place the microphone on the shirt and with different voices. Place the mic chest-high; if it is too close to the interviewee's mouth, voice distortion can result. Also, avoid placing it so far down the shirt that it records ambient room noise. If the subject wears a pullover shirt, there is no way to adjust the mic's distance from his or her mouth. Therefore, advise the Star to wear a button-up shirt or a jacket

We do not recommend hiding a microphone under clothing or you will have to contend with the clothing noise. When clothing physically rubs against or strikes the mic capsule or cable, it makes a loud, static noise. The microphone rubbing up against the clothing is one of the biggest sources of unwanted noise.

Although it is acceptable for the microphone to be visible to the audience, there is never an excuse for having a cable show; that is sloppy video work. We frequently just tuck the cord behind the chair or next to the chair's arm. Keep excess cords out of the shot wherever possible.

Specialty Microphone (for Smartphone, Compact Camcorders)

Audio on a smartphone often sounds like you are recording in a tunnel. A great solution to this problem is to add a microphone. You can configure a mic that you already own[14] or buy a pocket-sized specialty microphone. Here are some of the options available as of this writing.

Specialty microphones for smartphones and compact camcorders

Smartphone Video Tips

- Always shoot in the horizontal (landscape) orientation, with the smartphone on its side.
- Get in close. Frame the subject in a head-and-shoulders composition. This will also help with the audio.
- Consider buying an external mic for your smartphone.[15]
- When recording, block notifications, pre-set alarms, incoming calls, etc.
- Upgrade your video app. The default video apps are fine for taking a quick video in a well-lit area, but for a longer Life Reflections video, we recommend upgrading to an app that is easy to use and has video image stabilization, quality settings, and tap-to-focus features.
- Make sure you have enough free storage space. Video takes up a lot of storage space—around 100 MB per minute—so make sure you clean up your phone's storage or expand your memory with an additional microSD card if your smartphone has this capability.
- Use a mount or tripod. Smartphones require a specialty universal tripod mount that will attach to any tripod. Flexible tripods allow you to stabilize your camera in even the most cramped settings. The goal is to secure the smartphone at the interviewee's eye level.

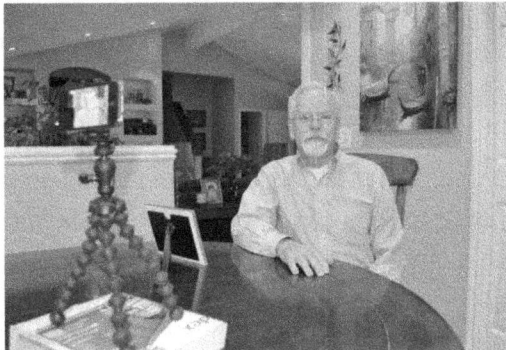

Adjustable tripod for smartphone

Light Your Path

Proper lighting is essential. Fortunately, this is usually easy to accomplish with little added equipment. We have found that lighting for a Life Reflections video is purely functional versus artistic. We simply seek pleasant lighting that lights the subject's face adequately.

Lighting professionals advise videographers to avoid mixed lighting, e.g., sunlight through a window mixed with artificial light. We have found, however, that different lighting combinations are adequate for the Armchair Interview. A few easy steps are all that is necessary to ensure that your Star is lit well with lighting you currently have.

Swivel the chair to face the window

Good video lighting is different from household architectural lighting. Architectural lighting nearly always points downward from the ceiling and usually casts deep shadows on the eyes and under the nose. Video lighting is aimed into the subject's face rather than down on the top of his or her head. This eliminates dark shadows and sends illumination into the eyes. Seeing the subject's eyes helps your viewers connect with him or her. Be sure to look at the video LED playback screen on your camcorder to review what the camera sees. Smartphones need more light than other types of video cameras.

Joan's house was built before three-prong grounded plugs were common and has not been updated. We made note of this during the initial setting evaluation and interview with Joan, so we were prepared with an adapter as well as a multi-outlet, heavy-duty power strip on recording day.

It is not important what your eye sees in the room; rather, focus on what the monitor on the camera sees, and adjust the lighting as needed. Each camera will have wide variations in how it captures light, and small adjustments will make a large impact in flattering your Star.

Window Light: Flaunt It if You've Got It

All light is an imitation of the sun. The reason that Hollywood does not always like to use the sun is that it is not completely reliable. Of course, we are not making a Hollywood video. You should work with what you have.

Set up the lighting the best that you can before bringing in the Star. Consider bringing in a friend or assistant to stand in for your Star during the lighting manipulation. You do not want to have your interviewee sitting around for long periods while the equipment is being adjusted.

Some of the best interview lighting is the light coming through a window. Natural outside light is usually diffused a bit, and you can use it. Just be sure your subject does not have his or her back to the window, which will cause the image to appear as a giant silhouette. Take advantage of existing natural light by locating the subject where sunlight will illuminate his or her face, and consider placing additional lights as needed.

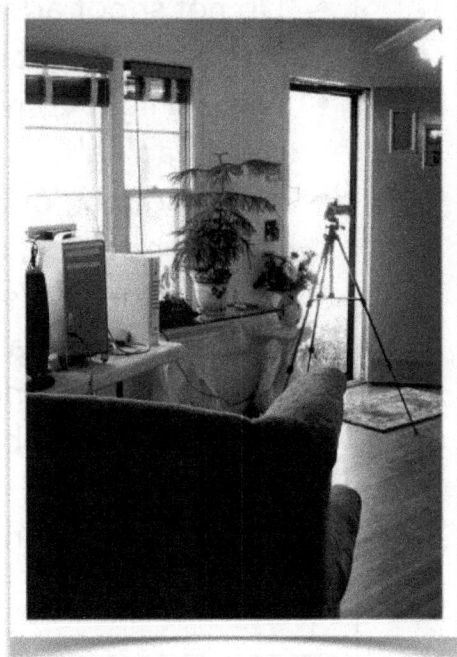

Swivel the chair toward a window to illuminate the subject's face.

Lighting is different in every situation. We try to place the chair at a slight angle toward the window. Placing a lamp on the opposite side of the Star provides flattering "fill" light, which balances the light on both sides of the face. If your Star's face is not illuminated adequately, you may need to move a light closer, swivel the subject, or move your camera. Lamps initially may not be powerful enough to illuminate the face, in which case a quick fix is to replace the light bulb with a higher wattage bulb or remove the lampshade. This creates a more powerful light and results in a much more flattering scene. Overhead lights usually are not desirable because they can create deep shadows on the face. If overhead lights are all you have available, you might be able to balance them with a reflector.

Lighting Tips

- Assess, and use, natural sunlight shining through windows and doors.
- Do not shoot against a window. Turn the chair around so the window lights the side of the Star's face.
- Natural light coming from a window is more flattering than overhead light.
- Add, redirect, or reduce artificial lighting with lamps, reflector boards, and lamp bulb wattage to balance the light on the Star's face.
- If your camera has a manual exposure button, use it to brighten the scene.
- Raise horizontal blinds to eliminate an undesirable striped shadow.
- Set up the lighting the best you can before bringing in the Star.

Light-Reflector Boards: Creative Household Substitutes

If you are limited to the available light, a reflector board can be a lifesaver. Any white or shiny surface can become another light source. Reflected light is not as noticeable as flipping on a light switch, but where you may not see a dramatic difference in the lighting with your eye, the camera's "eye" will.

Here are some common improvised reflectors:

- A white paper plate

- A windshield sunshade

- Stiff cardboard or foil-covered cardboard

- A whiteboard

• A survival blanket that is gold on one side and silver on the other

We also have propped a white three-ring notebook binder against a water pitcher that was on the kitchen table to direct lighting upward toward the Star's face, which worked beautifully. This added just enough light to reduce the shadows. Another easy and inexpensive option that we frequently use is a piece of white poster board purchased at the local dollar store.

Notice the posterboard propped in the chair to reflect window and lamplight onto the subject.

Following these technical tips will enhance your video recording. These technical details will prompt you to be prepared for various challenges you might face in recording a treasured Life Reflections video. However, please don't feel that you must be a master of audio and lighting to proceed. We have learned from the collective wisdom of dozens of beautiful older folks, and one prime lesson is *don't sweat the small stuff.* The true treasure is found in your loved one's thoughts and words.

To-do:

• Avoid surprises: Practice setting up and using your equipment.

Chapter Five:

IT'S A WRAP

Chapter Five

IT'S A WRAP

There are hundreds of paths up the mountain, all leading to the

same place, so it doesn't matter which path you take. The only

one wasting time is the one who runs around the mountain telling

everyone that his or her path is wrong.

~Hindu Proverb

"It's a wrap!" is what a director shouts when the shooting of a movie is successfully completed. This post-production chapter leads you through the technical considerations you will face as you decide how to prepare your video for viewing. You may choose to share the recording "as is" or enhance it through editing. You may opt to put the video on a DVD or post it to a social sharing website or archive to an on-line storage area. It is time to take the final video production steps on your personal path to creating a Life Reflections video heirloom.

The various conversion, viewing, editing, and saving details for smartphones and camcorders are explained in this chapter. Did you use a smartphone or a camcorder? Is your phone an Android or an iPhone? Will you edit your video or leave it uncut? Will you post the video online or burn a DVD? Your answers to these questions will dictate your formatting options.

Currently, the most common delivery method for video distribution is on a DVD, but that is quickly changing. We are far from the days when people watched commercially produced network television shows while sitting in front of the TV. Today, viewers watch videos produced from myriad sources, including content of varying lengths, on their computers, smartphones, and tablets, as well as on their TVs. The industry as a whole is trending toward sharing video online. Apple began removing DVD burners from portable computers years ago. The 2013 iMacs are the first desktop computers without optical drives. "These old technologies are holding us back," said Philip Schiller, senior vice president of worldwide marketing at Apple Inc. "They're anchors on where we want to go."[16]

Cloud computing is the next stage in the Internet's evolution. "In cloud computing, the word 'cloud' is used as a metaphor for *'the Internet,'* so the phrase *cloud computing* means 'a type of Internet-based computing."[17] Many different services such as video storage and video editing applications are delivered to computers and mobile devices through the Internet. The beauty of cloud-based video archives is that those who have been invited to view your video can access it whenever and wherever they want by entering the website URL into any Web browser (e.g., www.facebook.com, www.youtube.com). Social sharing websites such as Facebook, YouTube, and Vimeo and online cloud storehouses such as Justcloud, Moxy, and Dropbox offer personal storage space on the cloud. Most of these storage companies will host a short video (about five minutes) for free. Longer videos need more storage space and usually require a paid subscription. If your TV or Blu-Ray player is web-enabled, you can access and view video that has been stored on the cloud.

> Twitter is a new kind of collection for the Library of Congress but an important one to its mission. As society turns to social media as a primary method of communication and creative expression, social media is supplementing, and in some cases supplanting, letters, journals, serial publications, and other sources routinely collected by research libraries. [18]
>
> ~LOC Spokeswoman

If you used a smartphone to record a Life Reflections video, sharing your video online by posting to a service like YouTube, Facebook, or a similar site is the easiest option. Users who wish to share long videos on these sites simply divide their videos into ten-minute segments (e.g., part one, part two) before posting. Sharing online eliminates the need to mail multiple DVDs or flash drives, and it appeals to the current video-dominant generation. Today's youth send and receive short, original video clips routinely, and marketers realize the power of this media. Video sharing is even used in political elections to mobilize young people and connect with constituents. Twitter, which is an online social networking and microblogging service, recently added video sharing to its services. [19] There are dozens of other video hosting services such as Shutterfly where users can distribute their videos.

Posting your Life Reflections video online is fast becoming the most effective medium for engaging today's viewers as well as ensuring that future generations can access the stories of their ancestors easily. Over the past year, the number of people accessing video content online has increased by 38 percent, and the number of people accessing videos via smartphones has increased by 34 percent. People are using smartphones like televisions. More than half of smartphone videos are watched at home. And each week, a whopping 29 million people watch video from their smartphones; the average person watches five hours of video from his or her smartphone per week.[20]

Video transfer services are acknowledging the online trend. Customers of YesVideo automatically receive a private online Memory Save account for the videos they have converted to DVD. With that online account, customers can share their transferred footage easily through Facebook, Twitter, and e-mail to computers and mobile devices.

The majority of video cameras on the market today record video digitally with an electronic image sensor to a memory card rather than to tape or film. This change from mechanical and electrical technology to digital technology is referred to as the Digital Revolution.

The camera's digital data is encoded in a variety of ways, dependent on the camera's make and manufacturer. Your camera, whether camcorder, smartphone, or tablet, will initially save the video to a source file that contains minimally processed data from the image sensor of the digital camera. Similar to how negatives are used in film photography, the source files on your video camera will need to be 'developed' or converted into a viewable format. This data conversion may be automatically accomplished by your smartphone, by the DVD burner, or by the editing software. Once your files are converted into a popular digital format, your options for viewing, sharing, and saving are wide ranging.

> Your smartphone is a mini-computer which automatically converts your source data into files that are web-ready.

The following "Now What?" chart illustrates your options. Please locate your chosen path on the following chart to complete your final production tasks.

Now What? Smartphones and Camcorders

Burn a DVD	Reformatting	Viewing
	• Send memory card to a data conversion service. • Burn a DVD of files downloaded from the cloud with DVD player/burner. • Download files to a personal computer and burn a DVD. • Use a camera-to-DVD burner.	• Make multiple copies to share with family. • Watch video on TV or computer with a DVD player.
Cloud Sharing	• Publish files from smartphones and tablets directly to the cloud. • Download files to personal computer and share to cloud. • Send memory card to a data conversion service such as YesVideo, which will post the video to your account on its cloud-based Memory Share site.	• Watch video on YouTube, Facebook, or similar websites.
Directly from Device	• Use video connecting cables. • Burn a DVD with player/burner as it is viewed.	• Watch video on a mobile device. • Attach camcorder, smartphone, or tablet directly to TV for group viewing.

Save to a Flash Drive	• Download video files to a computer and save on a flash drive. • Send flash drive to conversion service for DVD burning.	• Insert flash drive into USB port on computer, television, or DVD player for group viewing.

Sharing Options

Burn a DVD

While it appears that technology is moving toward the cloud and away from optical disk technologies as of 2013, we like the idea of creating DVDs. We recommend them because the disks can be viewed without an Internet connection and a DVD provides an additional backup. Being able to hold and touch this special treasure fosters intimacy. Many houseolds in the United States have DVD players as part of a home entertainment system and/or on their computers. Burning a DVD can be complicated because it depends on your recording equipment and individual expertise, but you have several good solutions to consider if you are unable to use personal computer to create a DVD.

Panasonic, Canon, and Sony make camera-to-DVD burners for their cameras.

Camcorders can bypass the computer to burn an unedited video to a DVD by attaching a disc burner that interfaces directly with your camera. These convenient burners manage the necessary file conversion and burning processes needed to burn a DVD. Panasonic, Sony, and Canon offer DVD writers specifically for their cameras; additional conventional standard writers are also available. Sony sales representatives state that their burner connects with virtually any camcorder, VCR, or DVR and even accepts the four most common memory cards.[20]

DVDs are transferred in real time (e.g., a forty-minute recording will take forty minutes to transfer). A normal DVD holds about 4 gigabytes of data. Blu-Ray discs, the successor to DVD, usually hold 25 GB. The size of the video file depends on the quality settings on your camcorder. If the highest-quality setting is used, the DVD will hold about ninety minutes of video files. If you used an economy setting, the DVD will hold twice as much, but the playback quality will be visibly poorer.

Magnavox DVD player/burner HDD&DVD recorder with digital tuner

Another approach to burning a DVD without a computer is a multi-function Blu-Ray DVD player/burner. Most video that is posted online can be streamed to a Blu-Ray DVD player/burner on which a DVD can be burned simultaneously as the video is played. Consult your manual to confirm that your preferred video service is supported. Many of these units also accommodate video transferred directly from your recording device. Hook your camcorder to the video and audio ports on the back of the DVD player/burner to burn a DVD.

Compact camcorders and still cameras (SLR and point-and-shoot) shoot video and have removable memory cards.

Remove the battery cover to access memory card.

Finally, third-party companies will transfer video from your camera's removable memory card to a DVD. Camcorders record onto either a built-in hard drive or a removable memory card, so make sure to choose the memory card as the file destination when recording your Life Reflections video if you choose to use such a service. While camcorders produce several different video file formats that are manufacturer-dependent, file transfer companies are familiar with these formats and do an excellent job of converting them to DVD. Many popular camera departments (e.g., CVS, Walgreen's, Sam's Club, and Costco) and specialty camera stores such as Wolf/Ritz Camera and online conversion services can convert the files saved on memory cards. [22]

Android smartphones have removable memory cards that also can be processed through a conversion service. Consider purchasing an extra removable memory card that can be dedicated to the Life Reflections video project. Android devices support removable microSD or microSDHC memory cards with maximum capacities of 32 GB, which is plenty of room for a ten- to thirty-minute video. The memory card slot is located on the side or inside the back cover of the phone. It might, however, be located below the battery compartment.

As of this writing, video transfer companies are not equipped to download movies from iPhones or iPads because they do not have removable memory cards. The internal memory must be downloaded via a USB cable to a personal computer. If you do not have access to a computer, a specialty camera or computer store in your area might be able to download your iPhone. Once the video from your iPhone or iPad is transfered to a flash drive (also called a thumb drive or USB drive), then YesVideo or another video transfer service can use that flash drive to burn a DVD.

Share in the Cloud

Videos that are stored in the cloud can be viewed on your standard TV if it is web-friendly, or with a Blu-ray player that is web-enabled. Several TV manufacturers (e.g., LG, Vizio, Sony) are embracing standards for Internet-connected TVs. The units currently feature the Google TV platform that enables viewing of YouTube videos, websites, and more.[23] By 2015, analysts estimate, total shipments of wireless-ready TVs will reach 138 million worldwide.[24]

> Your smartphone is a mini-computer which automatically converts your source data into files that are web-ready.

One of the most popular social sharing sites is Facebook. Access the Facebook website through a web browser on your personal computer or download an app on your smartphone or tablet to create a personal account. The free Facebook app can be found at an online app store such as the Apple App Store, Google Play, or the Amazon App Store. Facebook's individual account settings allow you to define your audience based on your privacy settings. Once your video is online, it may be viewed, downloaded, and even edited at a later time. Using this online resource relieves you of the burden of duplicating and mailing DVDs and provides an additional backup of your prized recording.

One advantage of smartphones is that their built-in computers can access the software needed to convert your video source files into a web-friendly format before you post them to the cloud. The iPhone automatically converts to a web-friendly format, whereas some Android phones may require additional software for conversion. Facebook offers a special Video Uploader for Android. If you choose to share the video to a different online site, you will need conversion software tailored to the various Android file formats.[25]

View Directly from Recording Device

Connect your smartphone or tablet directly to your TV, and you can watch your video masterpiece on the big screen. You will need the proper conversion cables for your specific smartphone and TV. The specialized connectors hook up to the HDMI port on your TV and enable you to access videos from your smartphone's internal storage. Some TVs allow you to plug in a flash drive. Users of the iPhone and iPad can purchase an AppleTV, which does this with no cables (assuming a shared wifi network is present).[26]

If the emergence of easy, online video viewing on a big screen television inspires you to create a more polished Life Reflections video, take comfort in knowing that all of the conversion and sharing information previously discussed applies to your edited video, too.

Current flat screens have a USB port among the other plethora of plug-ins.

Mobile devices expand viewing options.

Editing the Video

Multimedia Life Reflections videos are beautiful to view and frequently awe-inspiring. The videos may include dramatic transitions, music, heirloom photographs, and text over-lays. Editing software also enables structural enhancements such as indexed "chapters" for easy viewing.

It is certain that your video recording will be cherished regardless of whether or not it is ed-ited. If your chosen path is to create an unedited video, you may have played music in the back-ground as you recorded and/or presented photos

Edit your video with a computer, a smartphone App or a cloud-based editor.

to the video camera as a method to include them without editing. You most likely chose an uncut path because of limited time, equipment, or editing expertise. The important thing is to be able to share and save the video you have carefully captured.

If you are comfortable with editing software, you will likely enjoy spending time editing your loved one's vid-eo and feel proud that you personally crafted this family keepsake. If you are new to video editing, we recommend that you shoot the video *now* and learn about editing lat-er. The original files saved on the camera's memory card (source files) should be saved and archived along with the converted files. By taking action now, you will have the option to go back and edit the video at your leisure and take comfort in knowing that your loved one's memory has been preserved.

It was an emotional experience to view Mother's video with her for the first time. I reached over to her and picked up her hand as we watched her life unfold on screen. I have never felt so much love and respect for the woman who raised me. I am so grateful to my older siblings for putting this together. Now that I am quite old myself, I intend to give my life as a gift on video to my children.[27]

~Peggy Castle

Cloud-Based Editing

Cloud-delivered applications tackle the barriers that typically prevent people from editing their video content: cost of purchasing editing software for an individual computer, complexity, and the need for heavy computing resources. The cloud provides access to free or low-cost video editing software directly from an Internet browser. The YouTube Video Editor allows you to create polished videos and upload them to their site, where they are available to share with family and friends. WeVideo is another online platform for collaborative video production in the cloud. Its online community enables you to edit and share video from any web browser. Your edits are stored and accessible online (www. wevideo.com), and if you choose to upgrade to an account that allows for more viewers and larger files, you may do so for a yearly cost.[28]

Personal Computer Editing Software

Many amazing video editing software programs are available today. To make things even better, both Windows and Macintosh operating systems come with their own basic video editing software (Apple's iMovie and Microsoft's MovieMaker).[36] MovieMaker creates .wmv files as the default output, while iMovie produces .mov files. If you are ready to make the move to a more full-featured film *editor*, Videomaker recommends Adobe Premiere Elements.[29]

To transfer videos from your camcorder to a personal computer, use a USB cable. If your camcorder records onto tape (an older technology), then that data will need to be converted to digital format. Refer to your camcorder's user manual to determine what type of connection you will need to transfer the video.

Videomaker

Go to www.videomaker.com to access in-depth information for creating and publishing great video.

Be aware that transferring video from a camcorder to a computer may consume a lot of hard-drive space. Consider transferring videos to an external flash drive or hard drive to save storage space. Be sure to close other running programs before the video is offloaded to your computer to preserve computing resources.

Smartphone/Tablet Apps

Editing apps are available for both platforms of smartphones and tablets; they enable you to edit video right on the device.[30] With editing software, you can trim off unwanted footage, stitch clips together, add fancy transitions, and insert royalty-free background music—all without a computer.[31] Often these applications are free and easy to find online. Apps for the Android include PowerDirector Mobile, a touch-optimized video editor for Windows® 8 tablets, Clesh Video Editor, and Google's built-in Movie Studio. Apple's iMovie is available to iPhone users, and Pinnacle Studio is accessible for the iPad. Be aware that copyrighted music cannot be posted to online websites. Video files are large and use up a lot of your phone's processing resources, so Android users should change the memory settings to allow video files to be stored on a memory card in the phone. Currently, iPhones do not have the capability to use a memory card, and the individual phone model dictates your storage capacity. Smartphones and tablets effortlessly convert source files into popular file formats that are easily uploaded to the web with the touch of a button.

While this chapter has presented a number of specialized technical concepts, almost assuredly by the time you read this, technology will have changed, and some newer, cooler invention will have been developed. It is our hope that this existing technology review gives you a sense of present-day editing, sharing, and archiving options.

www.harrycutting.com

Include still photos in two ways: display during video recording and/or digitize and insert into edited movie.

Digitizing Photographs

It is easy to include old photos within an unedited Life Reflections video by presenting them to the camera for recording during the on-camera interview. Ask your Star to hold them steadily in place for at least five seconds as he or she discusses the photo's subject.

If you plan to insert old photos into an edited Life Reflections video through editing, you must first digitize them to a .jpeg format. Converting vintage photos and video into a usable long-lasting digital format protects them from the effects of time and prepares them to be integrated into memorial presentations, multimedia Life Reflections videos, or other video scrapbook projects. You can use a scanner, a digital still camera, or a professional conversion service to digitize photographs.

Scanner

Many very good consumer scanners are available. We recommend scanning to 300 dpi (dots per inch) because this resolution is ideal for reprinting photos and results in manageable file sizes to e-mail and post online. Resolutions higher than 300 dpi or different file formats (such as TIFF, GIF, BMP, PNG, PSD, EPS) result in larger files than most people need. Furthermore, large files above 300 dpi can overwhelm your computer.

Remember to label all photographs with a photo-safe soft-tip pen. You may know who Uncle Harry is, but your children may not know in thirty years. Include full names and birth and death years where possible (e.g., Harry R. Black, 1890–1960).

Digital Still Camera (Camera Scanning)

Camera scanning provides an easy way to digitize old photos. Simply take a picture of your old photograph and import it into your editing software. Diffuse the lighting to avoid reflections or bright spots on your digital still; you will know immediately if you are satisfied with the results. If unsatisfied, simply retake. You can use your macro lens to capture specific people or zoom in on faces. Use a tripod or set the camera on a solid surface to keep the camera perfectly steady. Use the self-timer because even the act of pressing the camera button can cause movement and blurriness. To get a less distorted picture, place a heavy acrylic sheet on top of books or photos that won't lie flat.

Professional Conversion Services

Professional Conversion services can convert still photos and videotapes into a digital format. Many stores and online businesses offer bulk digitizing and correction services for still photographs. Video of times gone by adds a rich element to any multimedia tribute. If you have Super 8 films, VHS tapes, or other older media, you can transfer them onto more modern media (e.g., DVDs, hard drives, or the cloud) with the help of third-party services

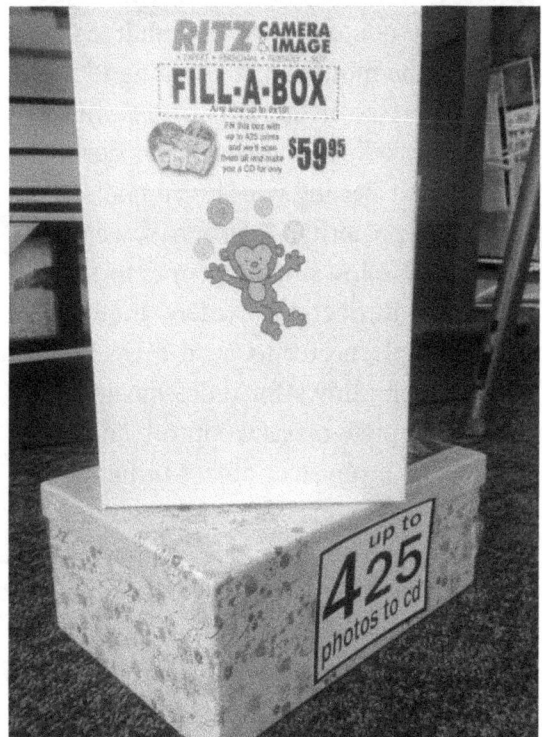

Camera stores such as Wolf/Ritz offer bulk digitizing services for photographs.

such as those available through CVS, Walgreen's, Sam's Club, Costco, specialty camera stores such as Wolf/Ritz Camera, and online conversion services. Alert the conversion service that if you intend to re-edit the converted video because additional steps may be needed to prepare the converted data for editing. YesVideo recommends that Mac users install the third-party application Handbrake, which converts DVD movies into an editable movie file. Intel computer users can edit those files without conversion. Once the files are on your computer, use your favorite video editing software to make your changes. The software user manuals will guide you on how to import your digitized photographs and video into your editing program on your personal computer.

Wrapping up your video through post-production may be as simple as uploading the unedited video from your smartphone to an online sharing service or as complex as editing a multimedia Life Reflections video on your personal computer. Regardless of the camera you used, or the editing path you choose, your audience is waiting.

Viewing Options

The Star's family and fans can access the video in many different ways. The Hindu quote "There are hundreds of paths up the mountain, all leading to the same place, so it doesn't matter which path you take" reminds us of our our ultimate goal: sharing your loved one's essence for posterity. A group screening celebration allows many people to view the Life Reflections video together. Many people prefer to burn a DVD to view, which allows for more music options*, complete privacy control, and the comfort of a physical object in hand. A video posted to one of the popular online

Video screening celebrations are important to the Star and to the people who care about them.

websites such as Facebook, Vimeo, or YouTube or saved to online storage site such as iCloud, air-Droid, Moxy, or Dropbox is a convenient way to share the video with family members who live far away and are unable to attend a group screening. Other options include distributing flash drives or written transcripts. The entire process of creating and sharing the video with your Star as the center of attention becomes a tribute to a life well lived.

*Most popular songs are copyrighted for personal use only. Online sites will not permit posting of a video which features restricted music. Use stock or royalty-free music if planning to post online.

Group Video Screenings

A live group video screening celebration features your Star's video on the big screen (when compared to the screens found on mobile devices or computer monitors). These events require a TV and a device on which to play the video. Most newer DVD players, Blu-Ray players, and TVs can access the Internet to play videos that have been uploaded to YouTube or similar sites. There are also easy ways to connect your smartphone or tablet directly to your TV. Regardless of the sharing method, approach your video screening with care.

Showing the video to a group requires careful attention and planning. Consider whom to invite and where to host the screening. The Star might say, "This is no big deal; I know what I said." It *is* a big deal—it is an emotional experience to hear and watch a loved one's life reviewed with future generations in mind.

Turn down the lights, remove distractions, test the viewing equipment, and keep the tissue boxes handy. Consider offering a light luncheon or dessert following the screening to celebrate the accomplishment.

One of our Stars chose to unveil her Life Reflections video at her eightieth birthday party. She said, "It was the highlight of the party and set a wonderful, positive mood for the entire reunion. I think that it reminded us all that life is fleeting and we need to make the most of every moment of every day."[32]

> I couldn't take my eyes off the screen. The music, the stories, the way one scene moved into another...but most of all, my mother on the video, almost as if she was in the room with me. I traveled with her through the stories of her life. This video is like having a favorite chat with my mother, but one that never has to end. I will always be able to have this visit with her, and I thank you so much for that.[33]
>
> ~Lori Ann Valley

One-on-One Screenings

Your Star may prefer to have one-on-one screenings with the special people in his or her life. The video will serve as an icebreaker for these sincere and very personal meetings in which life and death are often the topics. Whether your Star has been diagnosed with a terminal condition or is aging gracefully, the video will provide a centerpiece for these discussions.

There are many ways to share the video in a one-on-one setting. Perhaps you will sit side-by-side and view the video directly from your smartphone or tablet, download it to a television from the web or flash drive, or play a DVD. If you create a DVD or flash drive, make sure to have several copies to give away on these interpersonal journeys because everyone is sure to clamor for a copy after viewing it.

Protect Your Video: Save in Three Locations

Now that you have completed your Life Reflections video, you must store it securely to ensure that your video will last for generations. Store your data in three locations: Store the original source file and your converted file off-site—in a safe-deposit box, for example. Two copies, preferably on different types of media, should be stored at separate locations from the originals. The point is that if there were a fire or worse at your main location, you would still have two copies of all of your data stored safely somewhere else.

Always keep your source files. Source files are the files that your camera originally produced before editing or converting has occurred. Case in point: Many video enthusiasts transferred their home movies to VHS and now must save them to DVDS to view them because few people have retained the outdated VHS players. Unfortunately, video that is transferred from VHS to DVD is typically of poor quality. If those same people had saved the source files, they could be converted directly to DVD with far less degradation. The original uncut source files also may be useful in the future if you decide to create another edited video using different clips from the original footage. We recommend that you save the removable memory card from the camera, along with a copy the edited/converted video. The price of a new memory card is worth the assurance that an invaluable video heirloom will be preserved. Today's families most likely will not have shoe boxes containing old photographs of their ancestors. Instead, they will have DVDs, memory cards, hard drives, and cloud-based photo albums and video scrapbooks. This change to digital media takes effort, patience, and an unwavering focus on the ultimate goal: preserving your digital memories for children, grandchildren, and beyond.

Protect Your Videos:

1. Store the DVD and the related source file in a safe-deposit box or similar climate-controlled location.
2. Save video on a solid-state hard drive and migrate your videos as formats become obsolete. Make fresh copies every few years.
3. Save video on the cloud.
4. Establish an ongoing maintenance plan.

Sound daunting? Services certainly will be available in the future that will help you keep up with technology —just as there are services available today for transferring tape-based video formats onto DVDs. Just keep your eye on eye on the prize—preserving your family's memories.

Digital Video Discs (DVDs)

DVDs are an optical disc storage format with the ability to reproduce high-quality moving pictures and sound. They are durable and provide targeted access to individual movie segments. The downside is that if a disc gets scratched, it becomes unreadable.

The life span of CDs and DVDs is thought to be around fifty years. If you plan to use a DVD as your backup medium, it is well worth spending the extra money to buy top-grade branded discs. DVDs have between three and five layers of plastic and metal. How susceptible they are to damage depends on their construction. We suggest using archive-grade Gold Disks, which are designed to last much longer than standard DVDs.[34] As the laser reads

Store copies of your precious DVDs and hard drives in several different protected locations such as a safe deposit box.

through the layers, any damage—such as scratches, dirt, and finger—can interfere with retrieving data from the disc.

The best prospect for long-term retention of information on optical disks is regular copying and data migration. This means copying the information on the disk to a fresh disk or to another new technology format being developed. If you do this regularly, the information should survive indefinitely.[35]

Care and Handling of DVDs[36]

• Handle disks by the outer edge or the center hole only. Do not touch the surface of the disk.

• Disks should not be bent or flexed.

• Do not write or mark in the data area of the disk (the area the laser reads). Write on the clear "hub" area of the disk or, preferably, on the packaging that contains the disk. If you must label the disk itself, use a water-based felt-tip permanent marker to mark the label side of the disk. Do not use adhesive labels because the adhesive can damage the disk.

• Keep disks clean. If an optical disk becomes dusty, dirty, or fingerprinted gently remove loose dust using a non-abrasive photographic lens tissue or a very soft brush. Dirt can be removed using CD/DVD-cleaning detergent or isopropyl alcohol. The cleaning motion should never be circular (along the tracks). Always brush from the center of the disk outward. If a scratch is created while cleaning, it will do less damage cutting across the tracks than along them.

• DVDs should be stored at a stable temperature between 39° F (4°C) and 68° F (20°C) and relative humidity of 20 to 50 percent. In these conditions, natural deterioration can be slowed.

• Do not expose disks to prolonged sunlight or other sources of ultraviolet light. Fluorescent tubes are low in ultraviolet light, so use them wherever possible in storage areas. Storage areas should not have windows, but if they do, they should be covered with curtains or blinds.

• Store disks in their own rigid plastic cases. Remove a disk from its protective packaging only for use and return it immediately after use. Store disks upright (book style) in plastic cases designed for DVDs.

Computer and External Hard Drives

DVDs will eventually become outdated as well. The newer solid-state drives will likely last longer than DVDs, but as you notice new storage technology evolving, begin to transfer your video to the new storage media of the future.

Refresh digital archives on your computer or external hard drives at least every five years to stay current with format changes. Data stored and archived in a specific format today might not be readable twenty years from now because the technology used to read and interpret the stored bits could disappear.[37]

If you leave a hard drive on the shelf for a significant period of time, the lubricant in the bearings will degrade, and the drive may not spin up when you attempt to retrieve the data. To combat this, many people plug their backup drives in and run them once every six months.[38] The newest hard drives are solid-state hard drives and do not have moving parts. This means there are no mechanics to break, even when a machine is jostled or dropped. They are natively more resilient than hard disk drives.[40]

Online Storage (Cloud)

While we recommend posting your videos on the cloud for viewing and sharing, we also advise you to include two other backup media for long-term storage. If you are looking to store data for your lifetime, then online storage is a suitable option. If the intention is to preserve data for future generations, then we suggest that you employ multiple media sources, as discussed earlier. If you back up data using a free online storage account, your data is not secure. There is no guarantee that the company will not go out of business or begin charging for the service in the future—both circumstances that could lead to the deletion of your data.

Written Transcripts

A written transcript that converts the recorded spoken words onto a printed page is another way to protect the memories contained in your video project. You may choose to create this document yourself or ask a friend or family member to help. One note of caution: If you are not experienced at transcription, this process will undoubtedly take you longer than you expect. You may choose to hire a professional transcriptionist for longer video projects. We have found that transcriptionists charge between $75 and $100 per hour of video. Label and save your transcript in the same way as you do the video.

> Whenever I shoot video, before editing, I take the footage straight from my camera and store it on an external hard drive *and* my local computer. When I'm done editing, I have a finished movie file and all of the source files that came from the camera. Nothing ever gets deleted. I always keep two copies of those original source files in case I need them later, and they're safe if one of the hard drives ever dies.[39]
>
> ~Mike Wilhem, *Videomaker Magazine*

The devices and methods employed for keeping your data safe are varied, but the principle should always be the same: Any valued piece of computer data should *always* be stored on at least three physically different media, located in at least two distinct locations. You must also check all three and play the video yearly. Formats and techniques will change, but your diligent and dedicated determination will keep these treasures safe for future generations.

Video Storage and Archival Plan

Project name _____

	Store this plan with important papers such as your will and trust.	
Location #1 Safe deposit box	Location _____ Date _____ Name _____	Dates Viewed 2014 ☐ 2015 ☐ 2016 ☐ 2017 ☐ 2018 ☐ 2019 ☐
Location #2 External hard drive	Location _____ Date _____ Name _____	Dates Viewed 2014 ☐ 2015 ☐ 2016 ☐ 2017 ☐ 2018 ☐ 2019 ☐
Location #1 Cloud storage	Location _____ Date _____ Name _____	Dates Viewed 2014 ☐ 2015 ☐ 2016 ☐ 2017 ☐ 2018 ☐ 2019 ☐

Transcription Storage and Archival Plan

Transcription Project _____

	Store this plan with important papers such as your will and trust.
Location #1 Safe deposit box	Location _____ Date _____ Name _____
Location #2 External hard drive	Location _____ Date _____ Name _____
Location #3 Cloud storage	Location _____ Date _____ Name _____
Location #1 Acid-free scrapbook	Location _____ Date _____ Name _____

Chapter Six:

PARTING THOUGHTS

Chapter Six

PARTING THOUGHTS

A great biography should, like the close of a great drama,

leave behind it a feeling of serenity. We collect into a small

bunch the flowers, the few flowers, which brought sweetness

into a life, and present it as an offering to an accomplished

destiny. It is the dying refrain of a completed song, the final

verse of a finished poem.

~André Maurois

A "parting thought" is an ideomatic expression, a figure of speech. It is used to mean a last thought or a thought for others to ponder. Everyone has a parting thought to share. As photography affectionados, we personally advocate for capturing these parting thoughts in a formalized Life Reflections video. However, there are folks for whom such a video will never be accomplished, for various personal reasons. Please don't allow any resistance to recording a video become a "thorn" in your relationship with a beloved family member or friend. With today's technology, we have many ways to celebrate and record a person's life.

This chapter is an overview of how a memorial tribute can be accomplished posthumously as well as how hospice ambassadors can facilitate the creation of a simplified Life Reflection video using the easy Hospice Volunteer Method. Current technology enables anyone to capture, share and save important parting thoughts on video so there is no excuse for allowing a person to die without having captured their personality and essence on video for future. There is no excuse for allowing a person to die without having captured their personality and esssence on video for future generations.

Memorial Tributes

If a video has not been accomplished despite best intentions, it is not too late to honor a special person in your life. Even if you cannot capture a current video of your loved one, it is still possible to document his or her life and much of his or her personality with a memorial slide show. Historical photographs, audiotapes, and video can be set to music to create breathtaking memorial tributes. These memorial posthumous tributes provide a backdrop that helps the healing of surviving friends and family begin.

The Hospice Volunteer method uses this easy lighting setup: Position the interviewee's chair at a 45-degree angle from window.
Add a lamp to the unlit side if needed.

Memorial slide shows that honor the memory of a loved one are sometimes played in the reception area of a memorial service. We have found that a three- to five-minute slide show, automatically repeated or looped, is a comfortable length. We typically include thirty to fifty photographs and show each for five to seven seconds. Set over meaningful background music, the presentation is a gracious photo tribute appropriate for friends and family alike.

A nice touch is to overlay clear, explanatory text if possible. Identify personalities or places from the perspective of the person being honored. For example, name the person who gave birth to the honored one as "Maria Bowles, Mother "or "Grandfather's homestead in Black Hills, South Dakota." Photos organized in chronological order become a clear historical timeline for a "life story." The posthumous tributes are important for all attending. They are a wonderful way to mark the passing of loved ones.

A memorial slide show can also celebrate birthdays and anniversaries. We created an eightieth birthday tribute using the voices of the Star's children and grandchildren. We asked them to answer one question: "How do you know that your mom/grandma loves you?" The children and grandchildren, many of whom lived far away, submitted their responses by leaving their answers on a telephone answering machine. We captured that audio using a camcorder and, during the editing process, put a photograph of the messenger into the video. We took the responses that were submitted in written form and superimposed them in rolling text onto a photograph of the person who wrote the message. The finished product was compelling viewing for the grateful recipient. Although the creation of a memorial slide show is typically event-specific, you can create a Life Reflections video at any time. The quandary occurs when—as Gandhi said—"The trouble is, you think you have time." One of the biggest challenges is everyone's natural inclination to procrastinate.

The Hospice Effect

The Hospice Volunteer Method eliminates the need for a computer or editing: Send memory card from camera or smartphone to a conversion service.

People are inclined to think of events that are close at hand differently than those that are further away. Happenings that are close in time are seen as more concrete, and we tend to focus more on the details rather than on the big picture. Events that are further away are viewed as more abstract and do not result in motivation to act.

Often, we put these abstract desires on the back burner so that we can address current, more pressing situations. So if you are thinking about a goal that is a few years ahead (e.g., recording a video legacy before a loved one is gone), you can easily fall into woolly thinking instead of focusing on the concrete steps that will allow you to get there. We often hear people say, "Someday I am going to make a video of my mom explaining her immigration story" or "Wouldn't it be great if we were to turn on the video camera and ask Dad to talk about his childhood?" In our video

Hospice Volunteer Method (No computer or editing required)

1. Approach the patient with the opportunity to create a Life Reflections video.
2. Complete the Topic and Anchor Point Worksheet with the subject.
3. Gather all available recording equipment.
4. Record and have fun!
5. Upload the video to an online site or create a DVD. (Use a personal computer or send the camera's memory card to a conversion service.

recording practice, we regularly listen to people dream of what they will do "someday." We also hear those who have completed Life Reflections videos bemoan, "I wish I had done this sooner."

The "hospice effect" occurs when the hazy future is thrust into the present—when a person becomes ill and is moved into a hospice arrangement or is nearing the end of life. The future "to-do" list immediately becomes the "to-do *now*" list.

Hospice is not a particular place; rather, it is a service that aims to let people die comfortably and with dignity in their homes. Hospice nurses are skilled caregivers with the expertise and compassion necessary to provide quality care and comfort to the dying and their families. Unfortunately, many people mistakenly put off asking for hospice help soon enough. Overall, the median engagement with hospice is just twenty days, and almost one-third of patients enroll a week or less before they die.[41] "Nobody wants to say yes to death," Don Schumacher, president of the National Hospice and Palliative Care Organization, said. "America is a death-denying society, much more than others. And the health care system wants to continue to treat and treat and treat."

Regrettably, even if a physician signs the form stating that, in his or her best judgment, death is likely to occur within six months if the disease follows its normal course (the only form necessary to enroll in hospice), often it is the children who cannot bear to acknowledge that a father probably will not rebound this time or that a mother is dying. Therefore, they refuse to accept hospice care. Sometimes families don't want to hear the word "hospice." They might think that if they agree to allow a hospice servie to get involved, it means they are giving in and relinquishing hope. The irony is that hospice *provides* hope. It provides hope that a loved one will not experience pain and that he or she will live the remaining days surrounded by loving, caring people who understand his or her journey.

Hospice organizations work with a patient's primary care doctor. A hospice medical director also coordinates with families to send well-trained nurses to attend the patient, aides to lend a hand with daily care, and a social worker to help the family grapple with emotional difficulties and financial concerns. They will deliver needed equipment (a hospital bed or wheelchair) and supply pain-relieving drugs. Hospice organizations also employ chaplains and provide an on-call nurse who is available twenty hours a day to answer questions or solve problems that arise. We have worked with many different hospices and are awed by their compassionate expertise and amazed at the myriad resources they can bring to patients and families. For example, we created a Life Reflections video for a charming, teddy bear of a man whose hospice organization flew him and his nurse across the country to see his son receive a prestigious award.

We are hospice volunteers ourselves, and often our job is to stay with the patient while the family takes a much-needed break. It was actually during one of these visits that the idea for recording a Life Reflections video was born. We have seen firsthand the positive effect that recording a video legacy has on a dying person, and we are driven to share the "how to" because we have witnessed the sense of

peace and relief that overcomes people when the recording is finished. The look in their eyes and the smile on their faces seems to say, "Now I'm done. It is finished. I will not be forgotten."

Hospice nurses agree: Leaving a video legacy brings comfort and peace.

One of our clients commented after the recording, "I have a sense of closure." Her recorded words add permanence to her history. "It [the Life Reflections video] is done, and I feel better knowing that I've left my thoughts and my words behind." A hospice employee shared with us that she believes her patient lived longer because he wanted to complete the video. Experts agree with her: "Forming a story about one's life experiences improves physical and mental health," according to Dr. Kirsti A. Dyer.[42] A hospice patient and former nurse, Martha Keochareon, allowed herself to be interviewed shortly before her death. Her nurse said, "I notice that every time that Martha gave of herself, she received far more…. In fact, she received a few moments of less pain, and I suspect that she received life itself—a few more hours, even days, with purpose."[43]

It is arguably better to capture a Life Reflections video when a person is healthy and mentally alert. However, if a person has gotten this far in life and doesn't have a video recording that captures his or her essence, this is the last opportunity to leave a video legacy and a glimpse into his or her spirit. The process imparts peace for the dying person and can transform relationships.

When you record a Life Reflections video, it can be life changing for the interviewee as well as for others. We once met a gentleman named Gordon, a hard-hitting, skirt-chasing Navy veteran who drank too much. He had abandoned his family emotionally and physically after only a few years of marriage. When hospice called his daughter to inform her of Gordon's terminal condition, she had a hard choice to make: Would she ignore his condition the way he had ignored her for so long, or would she reach out to him? She chose to move him across the country to a nursing facility near her so that he wouldn't die alone. It was tense. Gordon was still a spirited, at times foul-mouthed sailor. When I posed the question "Did you ever chase any girls in the Navy?" he responded with a grin, "Yep, and I caught a few, too." His daughter noted that having a project to focus on allowed them to discuss the past in a less threatening atmosphere. They collaborated on his story topics and his shirt color. She even drove ten hours each way to collect old photos from his previous home to include in his Life Reflections video. Gordon died before his video was completed, but he accomplished the important task of reuniting with his daughter.

> Stories have to be told or they die. When they die, we cannot remember who we are or why we are here.[44]
>
> ~Sue Monk Kidd,
> The Secret Life of Bees

The creation of these videos provides families with a rare opportunity to clear the air and heal relationships. It allows individuals to set the record straight and to say those important words: "I'm sorry" or "I forgive you" or even "I love you" for the very first time. Every relationship we have been privileged to witness has been strengthened by the process. Kathie Supiano, an assistant professor at the University of Utah College of Nursing and the director of the college's Caring Connections: A Hope and Comfort in Grief program, said that old traumas often arise when one is dying. "Things bubble up to the surface that they have been able to keep under wraps. It's their last chance to be aired and voiced," she said. "This is something we need to be very attentive to and learn how to listen, how to allow thoughts and feelings and memories." The process heals and reveals and redeems. The process matters.

Dr. Ira Byock supported this idea, "I've lost count of the number of times I've met people in my office, an emergency room, or a hospice program who have expressed deep regret over things they wish they had said before a grandparent, parent, sibling, or friend died. They can't change what was, but without fail, their regrets have fueled a healthy resolve to say what needs to be said before it's too late—to clear away hurt feelings, to connect in profound ways with the people who mean the most to them."[45] While the creation of a Life Reflections video does not guarantee a solution to complex and fragile relationships, it is a powerful experience. The process provides a stage on which the dance of reconciliation can be performed. It is neutral ground where both parties can work together to complete the task before them. It requires mutual respect for one another's efforts and directs them toward a common goal. Life Reflections videos can be a good-bye that celebrates life.

We hope video scrapbookers and family historians everywhere will embrace this new and exciting way of looking at their loved ones' lives and legacies through the lens of a video camera. Whether you are a loving son or daughter or a hospice volunteer, you now have the tools you need to record a Life

Reflections video. It is truly in giving that you receive. The urgency of the Life Reflections projects is something that we feel every day because great lessons are too often left unsaid and unrecorded. We have met many wonderful people along our collective journey, and we have learned a great deal. So will you. Remember that, like photographs, memories do fade—and a Life Reflections video simply cannot wait until the "perfect time" because there is no such thing. *The perfect time is now.*

IMAGE SOURCES

Chapter One

"Dressing Room Star—Personalized," HTmart.com, accessed May 21, 2013, http://www.htmart.com/dressing-room-star-personalized.html.

"Camcorder," accessed May 21, 2013, http://www.turbosquid.com/FullPreview/Index.cfm/ID/447606.

"Compact/Pocket Camcorder. Pocket Camcorder on Tripod," Image title: image-gallery-4.jpg, Gorillapod Video, http://joby.com/gorillapod/video#images.

"Smartphone on Tripod," zdnet-joby-gorillamobile-tripod-iphone-4, accessed May 21, 2013, http://www.zdnet.com/blog/digitalcameras/joby-debuts-gorillamobile-tripod-for-iphone-4-39-95/4178. Associated article: Rachel King, Rachel. "Joby Debuts Gorillamobile Tripod for iPhone 4; $39.95."

"Still Camera with Video Capabilities," Freepik.com, accessed February 9, 2013, http://www.freepik.com/index.php?goto=41&idd=25644&url=aHR0cDovL3d3dy5zeGMuaHUvcGhvdG8vNTM2NDEw. 536410_photo_camera.jpg.

"Video Screenings Link Generations," last updated February 8, 2012, altered November 1, 2012, http://gooddev.com/how-to-maintainyour-tv-screen/. Associated article: Nick Jones, "How to Maintain Your TV Screen," last updated February 8, 2012.

Digital Knight Photography, "Father and Daughter Fishing," Permission granted by photographer Doug Havens. http://digitalknightphoto.wordpress.com.

Chapter Two

None.

Chapter Three

Fred Norton, Twyla Norton, and Janet Kinneberg Permission granted by photographer Pamela Clark.

Harry Cutting Photography, Inc., "Old Woman Holding Framed Picture of Deceased Husband," Photo C138-20. Model released. Permission granted by photographer. www.harrycutting.com.

Chapter Four

"Microphone Holes," accessed May 21, 2013. Associated article: Steve Morgenstern, "Canon EOS 7D Digital Camera Review," Reviewed.com, last updated December 16, 2009, http://www.digitalcamerainfo.com/content/canon-eos-7d-digital-camera-review-21327/video-features. Image name Canon_7D_Mic.

"Shotgun Microphone," Image number x143MKE400-F, http://www.crutchfield.com/S-Lm8DIevnpmm/p_143MKE400/Sennheiser-MKE-400.html.

"Camera-Mounted-Camcorder," image name: Sony NEX-VG30 Camcorder. Accessed May 21, 2013, http://fotostore.info/index.php?main_page=product_info&products_id=283. Image name: Sony NEX-VG30 Camcorder.

"Camera-Mounted-DSLR," Image name. 5d-with-rode-mic1-150x150. Associated article: "Video Accessories for the Canon 5D Mark II: Part 1—Microphones," http://dancarrphotography.com/blog/2008/11/30/video-accessories-for-the-canon-5d-mark-ii-part-1-microphones/.

"Lavalier," image name: sony-ecm-cs10-stereo-lavalier-microphone-ecmcs10-345x345. Accessed May 17, 2013, http://www.monstermarketplace.com/i-gadget-now-camera-accessory-store/sony-ecm-cs10-stereo-lavalier-microphone-ecmcs10.

"LiveAction Mic," accessed May 17, 2013, http://www.belkin.com/us/p/P-F8Z818.

Lyra Solochek, "Flip with Microphone," Gadgets & Gizmos, last modified September 21, 2010, accessed November 30, 2012. These materials are included under the fair use exemption and are restricted from further use. September 2010. http://www.tampabay.com/blogs/latest-gadgets/content/more-microphones-flip-cameras-smartphones-and-ipods.

Scott Merrill, "Close Up of Small iPhone Mic," image name: i-mic01. Last modified January 31, 2011. http://techcrunch.com/2011/01/31/review-gobiz-i-microphone/. Image name: i-mic01.

"Adustable Tripod with Smartphone. Smartphone on Tripod," image name: zdnet-joby-gorilla-mobile-tripod-iphone-4. Associated article: Rachel King, "Joby Debuts Gorillamobile Tripod for iPhone 4; $39.95," accessed May 21, 2013, http://www.zdnet.com/blog/digitalcameras/joby-debuts-gorillamobile-tripod-for-iphone-4-39-95/4178.

Lorraine Grula, image name: interview set up (3).jpg. Video Production Tips. http://videoproductiontips.com/using-natural-light-in-your-video-production. All content copyright 2007–2012.

Lorraine Grula, image name: interview set up (6).jpg, Video Production Tips. http://videoproductiontips.com/using-natural-light-in-your-video-production. All content copyright 2007–2012.

Chapter Five

"DVD," accessed May 21, 2013, http://soc82.com/order-reunion-dvd-cd.html. Image name DVD_disc.

"Flatscreen," image name: TV. http://wdmtech.wordpress.com/2012/05/19/lat-screen-tvs/.

"iPhone. Android Phone," image name: top-android-phones-nexus-4.jpg. Last modified December 7, 2012, http://blogs.computerworld.com/android/21462/top-android-phones-att-december-2012.

"Flashdrive," image name: Products838350-1200x1200-1072084.jpg. http://www.interstatemusic.com/838350-SanDisk-8GB-Cruzer-USB-2-0-Flash-Drive-SDCZ36A11.aspx.

Image name: VBDMA1, accessed May 21, 2013, http://store.sony.com/p/Blu-ray-Disc-DVD-Burner-Recorder/en/p/VBDMA1.

"Flatscreen," image name: TV. http://wdmtech.wordpress.com/2012/05/19/lat-screen-tvs/.

"Magnavox Burner," 500GB HDD&DVD Recorder with Digital Tuner, http://www.magnavox.com/product/feature.php?id=60.

"Nikon SLR Nikon D3200," image name: 25492_D3200_right.png. http://www.nikonusa.com/en/Nikon-Products/Product/Digital-SLR-Cameras/25492/D3200.html.

Jason Hidalgo (photo and article both). Image name: BlackBerry_Torch_04.jpg. Article title: "How to Replace a BlackBerry Torch Battery, SIM Card, or MicroSD Memory Card." http://portables.about.com/od/otherdevices/ss/How-To-Replace-A-Blackberry-Torch-Battery-Sim-Card-Or-Microsd-Memory-Card_4.htm.

"USB Back of TV," image name: TV-usb-sz-042710.jpg. http://www.apartmenttherapy.com/why-does-my-tv-have-a-usb-port-115428.

"Keyboard, Monitor, iPhone," image name: Dell screen monitor lcd keyboard mouse.jpg-c4cee24a-503f-448e-be4f-ce00b2278d22Large. http://www.turbosquid.com/3d-models/dell-lcd-monitor-keyboard-3d-model/596637.

"iPhone, Android Phone," image name: top-android-phones-nexus-4.jpg. Last modified December 7, 2012, http://blogs.computerworld.com/android/21462/top-android-phones-att-december-2012.

Videomaker logo.

"Old Woman Portrait," Stock Photo File #9704594, purchased from iStock photo.

Personal photo. Model released. Permission granted by photographer.

Personal photo. Model released. Permission granted by photographer.

"Safety Deposit Box," http://lostpedia.wikia.com/wiki/Safety_deposit_box. Safety_deposit_box.

Chapter Six

"Armchair," Stock Photo File #14865672. Purchased from iStockphoto December 2, 2012.

"Seniors Talking Together in the Living Room," Image ID #70312768, purchased from shutterstock.com. Signed model release filed with Shutterstock, Inc.

Image #39030212, accessed May 21, 2013, http://www.rakuten.com/th/hd-memory-card.html.

Image #42954281, accessed May 21, 2013, http://www.rakuten.com/th/hd-memory-card.html.

ENDNOTES

Foreword

Gautama Siddhartha (Buddha). 563–483 BC. Founder of Buddhism.

Introduction

1. Barbara Okun and Joseph Nowinski, *Saying Goodbye: A Guide to Coping with a Loved One's Terminal Illness*. (New York: The Berkley Publishing Group, 2011).

Patajali (Devangar) is the compiler of the Yoga Sutra, an important collection of aphorisms on yoga practices. http://thinkexist.com/quotes/patanjali/. Accessed January 16, 2013.

Gautama Siddhartha, ibid.

Chapter One

Gautama Siddhartha, ibid.

2. Kirsti A. Dyer, MD, MS, FAAETS, "The Importance of Telling (and Listening) to the Story, last modified December 6, 2001, accessed July 7, 2012, http://www.journeyofhearts.org/kirstimd/tellstory.htm.

3. Homer, *The Odyssey*, reissue edition. (New York: Penguin Classics, October 31, 2006).

4. Barbara K. Haight and Barrett S. Haight, *The Handbook of Structured Life Review*, Volume 2001. Health Professions Press; first edition, October 29, 2007).

5. Julie Bosman, "After 244 Years, *Encyclopaedia Britannica* Stops the Presses," last modified March 13, 2012, accessed December 5, 2012, http://mediadecoder.blogs.nytimes.com/2012/03/13/after-244-years-encyclopaedia-britannica-stops-the-presses/.

6. Margaret Rouse, "Camcorder (Camera Recorder), March 2009," accessed January 16, 2013, http://searchmobilecomputing.techtarget.com/definition/camcorder.

7. Kevin Lee, "This Is the First Full-Length Movie Filmed with a Smartphone," last modified November 30, 2011, http://www.techhive.com/article/245212/this_is_the_first_full_length_movie_filmed_with_a_smartphone.html.

8. Kimberly Yeamans (daughter of Life Reflections video subject David Yeamans), in discussion with the author, December 12, 2011.

Chapter Two

Hector Hugh Munro, Burman-born English novelist and short-story writer (under pseudonym Saki), 1870–1916), accessed October 10, 2010, http://thinkexist.com/search/searchquotation.asp?search=find+yourself+a+cup&q=author%3A%22H.+H.+Munro%22.

9. Paulette Stevens, "How Will You Be Remembered?" Utah Association of Personal Historians, last updated September 2012, accessed October 6, 2012, http://utahaph.blogspot.com.

Chapter Three

North American Indian proverb. http://www.wisdomcommons.org/wisbits/6030-tell-me-a-fact-and-i-ll-learn.

10. K. J. Doka, *Living with Grief: Loss in Later Life*, first edition. (Washington, DC: Hospice Foundation of America, January 15, 2003).

Chapter Four

11. Leonard Cohen, lyrics from "Anthem," accessed January 16, 2013, http://www.leonardcohen.com/us/music/futureten-new-songs/anthem.

12. "Microphones," CBS Interactive Inc., accessed December 2012, http://reviews.cnet.com/microphones/?filter=500908_501216_.

13. "Lavalier," last modified June 4, 2012, http://en.wikipedia.org/wiki/Lavalier.

14. "Simple with Styme. How to Put an External Mic on Your Smartphone." YouTube, last updated July 15, 2011, http://www.youtube.com/watch?v=2IAMgAzufNQ.

15. Justin Sevakis, "Use an External Microphone with the iPhone," last updated May 4, 2009, accessed November 9, 2012, (http://hints.macworld.com/article.php?story=20090501144335832).

Chapter Five

Hindu proverb. http://www.motivationalquotesabout.com/quotes/there-are-hundreds-of-paths-up-the-hindu-proverb.aspx. Accessed 8 July 2013.

16. H. McCracken, "Apple's Phil Schiller on the State of the Mac," last modified October 26, 2012, accessed February 13, 2013. http://techland.time.com/2012/10/26/apples-phil-schiller-on-the-state-of-the-mac/.

17. D. Murphy, "Library of Congress Twitter Collection: 170 Billion Tweets Strong," last updated January 5, 2013, accessed January 15, 2013, http://www.pcmag.com/article2/0,2817,2413889,00.asp.

18. "How to Share Video Using Twitter," last updated August 4, 2009, accessed March 16, 2013, http://www.twitterpowersystem.com/blog/how-to-share-video-using-twitter.

19. Taylor Martin, "Are You Watching More Video Content from Your Smartphone?" last updated May 30, 2012, accessed February 13, 2013, http://www.phonedog.com/2012/05/30/are-you-watching-more-video-content-from-your-smartphone/.

20. http://store.sony.com/p/Blu-ray-Disc-DVD-Burner-Recorder/en/p/VBDMA1. Accessed 8 July 2013.

21. http://www.yesvideo.com/default.aspx. YesVideo is the global leader in video transferring and sharing. The company's patented technology allows it to transfer personal videos efficiently. Customers may then view, edit, and share their videos in the cloud.

22. "Cloud Computing," Webopedia, accessed March 11, 2013, http://www.webopedia.com/TERM/C/cloud_computing.html.

23. Kothari Suveer, "Bringing More Entertainment to Your TV," last updated January 4, 2013, http://googletv.blogspot.com/.

24. Tony Gomez, "Getting Video to Your Smart Device in Three Steps," last updated October 10, 2012, accessed February 23, 2013, http://www.videomaker.com/article/15633-getting-video-to-your-smart-device-in-three-steps.

25. Yogesh Mankani, "Eight Best and Free Video Streaming Apps for Android Phones," last updated August 14, 2010, accessed February 23, 2013, http://savedelete.com/best-free-android-video-streaming-apps.html.

26. "How to Watch Videos from Your Smartphone or Tablet on Your TV," *Your Guide*, Verizon, last updated May 25, 2012.

27. Peggy Castle (daughter of Life Reflections video subject Paula M. Yeamans), in discussion with the author, April 24, 2013.

28. We video website, http://www.wevideo.com.

29. Colin Marks, "Adobe Premiere Elements 11 and Photoshop Elements 11 Video and Photo Editing Software," last updated March 2013, accessed April 30, 2013, http://www.videomaker.com/article/16012.

30. Emily Price, "Nine Apps for Editing Video on Your Smartphone," Mashable.com, last updated July 25, 2012, http://mashable.com/2012/07/25/video-editing-apps/.

31. " Power Director Mobile," Cyberlinklcom, accessed February 23, 2013, http://www.cyberlink.com/products/powerdirector-metro/overview_en_US.html?&r=1.

32. Berta Clark, subject of a Life Reflections video. in discussion with the author, September 22, 2012.

33. Lori Ann Vallen (daughter of Life Reflections video subject Lillian Bowlby), in discussion with the author, May 12, 2009.

34. Iovana Milutinovich, "How to Choose CD/DVD Archival Media," last modified January 11, 2013, accessed January 16, 2013, http://adterrasperaspera.com/blog/2006/10/30/how-to-choose-cddvd-archival-media.

35. "X Lab: Optical Media Longevity." Thexlab.com, accessed October 4, 2012, http://www.thexlab.com/faqs/opticalmedialongevity.html.

36. "Preserving CDs and DVDs," National Archives of Australia, http://www.naa.gov.au/records-management/agency/preserve/physical-preservation/CDs-and-DVDs.aspx.

37. SNIA is the Storage Networking Industry Association. It advances IT technologies, standards, and education programs for all IT professionals. Made up of some four hundred member companies spanning the global storage market, SNIA connects the IT industry with end-to-end storage and

information management solutions. The association is composed of several special-interest groups, including Cloud Archive and Preservation.

38. Mic Thornton, "Backing Up & Archiving Sessions," last updated July 2007, accessed October 2, 2012, http://www.soundonsound.com/sos/jul07/articles/protools_0707.htm.

39. Mike Wilhelm, *Videomaker* magazine. In discussion with author. 2 February 2013.

40. Christopher Barnatt, "Computer Storage," Explainingcomputers.com, last modified September 13, 2012, accessed November 1, 2012, http://www.explainingcomputers.com/storage.html.

Chapter Six

André Maurois, "Famous Quotes about Biography," accessed January 16, 2013, http://www.ranker.com/list/notable-and-famous-biography-quotes/reference.

41. Kristen Moulton, "Utah Workshop to Train End-of-Life Care Providers to Treat Veterans," *The Salt Lake Tribune*, last updated April 8, 2013, http://www.sltrib.com/sltrib/news/56112137-78/veterans-war-care-dying.html.csp.

42. Kirsti A. Dyer, MD, MS, FAAETS, "The Importance of Telling (and Listening) to the Story, last modified December 6, 2001, accessed July 7, 2012, http://www.journeyofhearts.org/kirstimd/tellstory.htm.

43. Abby Goodnough, "As Nurse Lay Dying, Offering Herself as Instruction in Caring," last modified January 10, 2013, accessed January 15, 2013, http://www.nytimes.com/2013/01/11/us/fatally-ill-and-making-herself-the-lesson.html?pagewanted=all&_r=1&.

44. Sue Monk Kidd, The Secret Life of Bees, reprint edition. (New York: Penguin Books, August 20, 2008).

45. Ira Byock, *The Four Things That Matter Most*. (New York: Free Press, March 2004).

BIBLIOGRAPHY

"2013 External DVD Burners Product Comparisons." Top Ten Reviews. http://external-dvd-burner-review.toptenreviews.com/.

@digitaltrends on Twitter, digitaltrendsftw on Facebook.

"A Five-Year Global Market Forecast" Pyramid Research. Mobile Video Services. Last updated May 2009. Accessed March 2, 2012. http://www.pyramidresearch.com/store/RPMOBILEVIDEOSERV0906. htm.

Anders, Jane. "The Wrong Way to Plan for the Future." io9.com. Last modified March 23, 2012. Accessed March 20, 2013. http://io9.com/5912199/the-wrong-way-to-plan-for-the-future

Baguley, Richard. "The New HD Camcorder Format Explained." http://pcworld.about.net/news/Jul272006id126518.htm.

Bea, Francis. "Video Conversion Service YesVideo Can Now Send Your Preserved Memories to Facebook Timeline." Digital Trends. Last modified October 18, 2012. http://www.digitaltrends.com/home-theater/yesvideo-facebook-timeline-integration/#ixzz2KibLvOFW.

Broida, Rick. "Don't Shoot: Ten Tips to Avoid Bad Home Video." Last modified September 17, 2004. http://reviews.cnet.com/4520-6500_7-5510172-1.html.

Byers, Fred. "Care and Handling of CDs and DVDs—A Guide for Librarians and Archivists." NIST Special Publication 500-252. Co-published by Council on Library and Information Resources and National Institute of Standards and Technology. October 2003.

"Camcorder Buying Guide." Last modified November 7, 2012. Accessed January 29, 2013. http://reviews.cnet.com/camcorder-buying-guide.

"Camcorder vs. Smartphone: Interchangeable for Video? eHow.com. http://www.ehow.com/info_12223993_camcorder-vs-smartphone-interchangeable-video.html#ixzz2JItZN8aS.

Carroll, Tom. Better Smartphone Video Sound -- Five Microphone Options. http://vimeo.com/37708595. Accessed January 29, 2013

Cassidy, Kyle. "What's the Best Video Format?" Last modified March 2012. Accessed January 29, 2013. http://www.videomaker.com/article/153621.

Cassidy, Kyle. "Popular Video Formats, Players, and Distribution Methods." Last modified January 1, 2010. Accessed January 29, 2013. http://www.videomaker.com/article/14519.

Cassidy, Kyle. "Basic Video Editing," last updated October 2009, accessed February 23, 2013, http://www.videomaker.com/article/14223.

CNET TV. http://cnettv.cnet.com/still-cameras-shooting-great-video/9742-1_53-50105536.html.

"Digital Camcorder Conversion: How It Works." Timeless DVD. Accessed January 25, 2013. http://www.timelessdvd.com/video-conversion/dvd-video-conversion.html.

Dixon, Doug. "Consumer Video Editors." Last modified January 9, 2013. Accessed February 13, 2013. http://www.videomaker.com/article/15707-consumer-video-editors.

Dumaplin, Beata. "A Brief Look into Video Editing for Mobile Devices." Last modified May 9, 2012. Accessed February 14, 2013. http://www.videomaker.com/videonews/2012/05/13718-a-brief-look-into-video-editing-for-mobile-devices.

Dyer, Kirsti A., MD, MS, FAAETS. "The Importance of Telling (and Listening) to the Story." Last modified December 6, 2001. Accessed July 7, 2012. http://www.journeyofhearts.org/kirstimd/tellstory.htm.

Eaton, Kit. "Tools of the Trade for the Smartphone Cineaste." Last modified February 6, 2013. Accessed February 14, 2013.

Gorg, Virginia. "The Best Ways to Store DVDs." http://www.ehow.com/way_5192369_ways-store-dvds.html#ixzz2EOcXyVCO.

Gruncy, Jeff. "How to Convert Camcorder Video to DVD." Accessed January 29, 2013. http://www.ehow.com/how_5807928_convert-camcorder-video-dvd.html.

Hoffman, Paul. "Camcorder Feature—Video Formatting and Editing." Panasonic. Last modified May 4, 2012. Accessed January 29, 2013. http://www.youtube.com/watch?v=v1MRywfn_7s.

"How to Convert Camcorder Video to DVD." eHow.com. http://www.ehow.com/how_5807928_convert-camcorder-video-dvd.html#ixzz2IvZUCkZ.

"Simple with Styme. How to Put an External Mic on Your Smartphone." Last modified July 15, 2011. http://www.youtube.com/watch?v=2IAMgAzufNQ.

McNamara, M. "Video DSLR Basics for Photographers. A Still Photographer's Guide to HDSLR Technology, Terms, and Features." Last modified August 22, 2011. http://www.adorama.com/alc/0012762/article/Video-DSLR-Basics-for-Photographers.

Marks, Colin. "Storage Buyer's Guide: Safeguarding Your Digital Creations." Last modified January 2013. http://www.videomaker.com/article/15750-storage-buyers-guide-safeguarding-your-digital-creations.

Martin, Jim. "Video Formats for Cell Phones." Last modified January 1, 2010. Accessed January 29, 2013. http://www.videomaker.com/article/14520.

"Panasonic HC-V700 Camcorder Overview." Accessed January 29, 2013. http://www.pcmag.com/article2/0,2817,2408404,00.asp

Prince, Sal. "Top 10 DVD Recording (or Burning) Software Programs." About.com Digital Video Recording. http://dvr.about.com/od/capturetvwithacomputer/tp/dvdrec.htm.

"Recorder with Digital Tuner." Magnavox.com. http://www.magnavox.com/product/feature.php?id=60.

Rouse, Margaret. "Smartphone." Last modified June 2007. Accessed November 14, 2012. http://searchmobilecomputing.techtarget.com/definition/smartphone.

Scoblete, Greg. "Guide to Camcorder Video File Formats." http://camcorders.about.com/od/camcorders101/a/camcorder_video_file_formats.htm.

Scoblete, Greg. "A New Image Sensor and Wide-Angle Lens for the V700." http://camcorders.about.com/od/buyingguide/a/Panasonic-Hc-V700-Camcorder-Overview.htm.

Sniadak, Dave. "YouTube Refines Memories." Last modified October 1, 2011. Accessed February 14, 2013. http://www.videomaker.com/article/15529.

Scoblete, Greg. How to Archive Camcorder Videos. Accessed December 7, 2012. http://camcorders.about.com/od/saving/a/archive_camcorder_videos.htm.

Siddhartha, Gautama (Buddha). 563–483 BC. Founder of Buddhism.

Smith, Christine. "Camcorder Tips." Last modified December 26, 2012. Accessed January 29, 2013. http://www.wondershare.com/dvd-burner/convert-camcorder-video-to-dvd.html.

Smith, Christine. "How to Transfer Camcorder Video to DVD." Last modified December 26, 2012. Accessed January 29, 2013. http://www.wondershare.com/dvd-burner/convert-camcorder-video-to-dvd.html.

Smith, Christine. "How to Transfer Videos from Camcorder to Computer." Last modified June 4, 2013. http://www.wondershare.com/camcorder/transfer-camcorder-video.html.

Sullivan, Terry. "The Best Still Cameras for Shooting Video." Last modified May 12, 2006. Accessed October 10, 2012. http://www.pcmag.com/article2/0,2817,1960909,00.asp.

"The Most Important Things to Know about Buying a Camcorder." Last modified November 7, 2012. Accessed January 28, 2013. http://reviews.cnet.com/camcorder-buying-guide/.

Thornton, M. "Backing Up & Archiving Sessions." Last modified July 2007. Accessed June 1, 2012. http://www.soundonsound.com/sos/jul07/articles/protools_0707.htm.

Zangaro, S. "Archiving and the Cloud." The Register. Last modified November 1, 2011. Accessed August 5, 2012. http://www.theregister.co.uk/2011/11/01/snia_cloud_archive_best_practices/.

YouTube. http://support.google.com/youtube. Accessed January 29, 2013.

www.ingramcontent.com/pod-product-compliance
Lightning Source LLC
La Vergne TN
LVHW061225060426
835509LV00012B/1426